HOW TO BUY THE RIGHT SMALL BUSINESS COMPUTER SYSTEM

More than a million people have learned to program, use, and enjoy microcomputers with Wiley paperback guides. Look for them all at your favorite bookshop or computer store:

BASIC, 2nd ed., Albrecht, Finkel, & Brown
BASIC for Home Computers, Albrecht, Finkel, & Brown
TRS-80 BASIC, Albrecht, Inman, & Zamora
More TRS-80 BASIC, Inman, Zamora, & Albrecht
ATARI BASIC, Albrecht, Finkel, & Brown
Data File Programming in BASIC, Finkel & Brown
Data File Programming for the Apple Computer, Finkel & Brown
ATARI Sound & Graphics, Moore, Lower, & Albrecht
Using CP/M, Fernandez & Ashley
Introduction to 8080/8085 Assembly Language Programming, Fernandez & Ashley
8080/Z80 Assembly Language, Miller
Personal Computing, McGlynn
Why Do You Need a Personal Computer?, Leventhal & Stafford
Problem-Solving on the TRS-80 Pocket Computer, Inman & Conlan
Using Programmable Calculators for Business, Hohenstein
How to Buy the Right Small Business Computer System, Smolin
The TRS-80 Means Business, Lewis
ANS COBOL, 2nd ed., Ashley
Structured COBOL, Ashley
FORTRAN IV, 2nd ed., Friedmann, Greenberg, & Hoffberg
Job Control Language, Ashley & Fernandez
Background Math for a Computer World, 2nd ed., Ashley
Flowcharting, Stern
Introduction to Data Professing, 2nd ed., Harris

HOW TO BUY THE RIGHT SMALL BUSINESS COMPUTER SYSTEM

C. ROGER SMOLIN

San Diego Business Systems

John Wiley & Sons, Inc.
New York • Chichester • Brisbane • Toronto

Library of Congress Cataloging in Publication Data

Smolin, C. Roger, 1948–
    How to buy the right small business computer system.

    Includes index.
    1. Business — Data processing. 2. Small business —
Data processing. 3. Computers — Purchasing. 4. Mini-
computers — Purchasing.   I. Title.
HF5548.2.S614   001.64'04'0687   81–4276
ISBN 0-471-08494-8   AACR2

Printed in the United States of America

81 82 10 9 8 7 6 5 4 3 2 1

TO MARSHA

Who convinced me that I should,
and could, write this book.

Permission to draw material from the following is gratefully acknowledged:

"Computers — The Plain Truth," C. Roger Smolin. Reprinted by permission of INTERFACE AGE, ©, November 1979.

"How to Buy an Accounts Receivable System," C. Roger Smolin. Reprinted by permission of INTERFACE AGE, ©, March 1980.

PREFACE

WHO SHOULD READ THIS BOOK

Although references in this book to the small business person may conjure up visions of little flannel-suited executives carrying tiny briefcases, this is not at all for whom this book has been written. I have arbitrarily defined a small business as one with from $0 (really small) to about $10 million annual gross sales. This book is for those who find themselves to some degree either out of control in their business or having to invest too much of their precious resources to maintain control.

But this, after all, is the nature of small business. "I do it all myself, but I *have* to do it all myself." And if you don't actually do it all yourself, you have to know how to do it or how to train somebody else to do it. (Then you must worry about whether it's being done right.)

By now, you have probably gotten wind of a miracle in the otherwise arcane and incomprehensible world of computers — that is, the age of the personal computer is here (or else you wouldn't be reading this book, would you?). And furthermore, you are told that small, inexpensive computer systems are now available to businesses like yours. Naturally, from the hype and PR that has accompanied this event, you are eager to participate. The cost/benefit ratio seems almost too good to believe. Well, guess what? It may be.

WHAT I'D LIKE TO DO FOR YOU

Because of the type of problems associated with the fledgling industry of small business computer systems (described more fully in Chapter 1), it may be difficult for you, as a first-time user, to successfully bring one of these systems into your business. I have witnessed and participated in this problem time and again. Still, I believe in the value of the computer in the very real advantages it can bring to the small business environment.

If you don't have to know how to design a car to buy one, why, for heavens sake, should you have to study computer systems before you buy and use one? Well, strictly speaking, you shouldn't have to. And 20 years from now, when the industry matures, you probably won't have to. But for now, knowing the language of data processing and a little about systems design will help your chances for success in business. This book will therefore outline how a computer works and how to shop for the equipment and programs you'll need for a small business system. It will explain in lay terms how the complex programming provided by the manufacturer is supposed to work and what features you should look for.

But most importantly, this book will outline the design of small business systems and show you how they should operate, what you should expect, and what you'll have to put into them to obtain something of value.

All of the above will be done, I hope, in clear, nontechnical language. I will assume that you know your debits and credits, what an inventory is, what accounts receivable and payable are; in short, that you have a fundamental business knowledge and vocabulary. I will also assume that you know nothing at all about computers.

BUT FIRST, A WORD ABOUT GENDER

I have concluded that the use of the generic "he" is no longer acceptable in society. I have opted instead for the infinitely more awkward "he/she," "his/her," "businessperson," and the like. Yes, I know, computers don't have genders but people do. But, the change in our language has to start somewhere.

Besides, I'll bet you didn't know that Cobol (the Common Business–Oriented Language), which is to data processing what Hebrew is to religion, was invented by a woman, Captain Grace Murray Hopper.

CONTENTS

1

INTRODUCING
THE COMPUTER

WHY A COMPUTER?

Doing more with less. This sums up what has been one of the primary yard-sticks by which humanity has measured its progress across the broad sweep of history. At first we spent all our time hunting and gathering. The organization of people into towns and cities and the domestication of crops and livestock meant that not everyone had to work all the time to eke out an existence. Specialized trades and professions appeared. As the number of people increased, so did the amount of goods and services each person contributed, aided by an increasing array of tools and other mechanical devices.

This trend reached a fever pitch in the eighteenth century, with the harnessing of water and steam power and the rudimentary applications of electricity. Great mills humming with machinery turned out products at a prodigious rate. Factories produced manufactured articles by the gross. Items regarded as luxuries to previous generations became commonplace. The sophistication of mechanical fabrication increased even more during the Second World War.

But let us leave the orderly din of the production floor and go to the front office for a moment, shutting out the sound of the ever more efficient machines. Let's visit with the people who are coordinating the myriad activities that make the wheels of industry turn.

And there our eyes are met by a most incongruous sight. Why, it's like stepping back 200 years. Armies of clerks carry reams of paper to battalions of scribes who make tiny marks on great ledger sheets in much the same fashion as cunieform marks were pressed into clay tablets 5,000 years earlier. These marks, representing numbers, pieces of inventory, sales records, and other vital management information, are collated, summarized, and reported — accumulating along the way as many errors as human beings are prone to make when performing boring, repetitive tasks requiring great accuracy and unflagging attention.

And what is the purpose of all this activity? Why, it's done to symbolically represent every activity going on in the real world of the production floor, the suppliers, and the marketplace, so that a manager can "see" the business on paper.

Management is overjoyed to receive these figures. Imperfect as they are, they are the only way to know what's been happening on the production floor and in the sales department and how much was spent on raw materials for the last week, month, or maybe 2 months. And it is based on this information, this imperfect view of the industrial process, that management makes its decisions; management is, in effect, working in the dark.

So, while technology has freed the laborers from much of their drudgery and increased productivity many times over, the accounting and reporting of these data — the tools that management requires to aid them in their decision-making process — are still in a primitive state.

Meanwhile, in the engineering department, the hush of genius is broken only by the clack of slide rules as the engineers struggle to calculate to three significant figures problems of technology that require much greater precision. And back at the universities, which turned out the engineers, mathematicians are accumulating problems that cannot be solved for sheer lack of calculating power. Scientists and researchers are unable to discover fundamental correlations, being faced with years of tedious calculations that may or may not yield significant results.

While we were able to invent machines to replace people at the most complex and intricate of mechanical tasks, there was still no way to *manipulate the symbols* that represented these tasks, to automate the *decision-making process* of a single person, or to figure out gross profit without a lot of tiresome, expensive labor. What was needed was a tireless, quiet, efficient device to replace the drudge tasks of the human brain.

IN THE BEGINNING. . .

Chances are that J. P. Eckert and J. W. Mauchley are not names that you have heard before or are likely to hear again. Then again, perhaps when computers are as important to all of us as the electric light, automobiles, or radio, Eckert and Mauchley will be as well known as Edison, Ford, and Marconi. In 1946 they gave the world its first electronic computer. In a lab in the Moore School of Engineering, University of Pennsylvania, they assembled a machine 100 feet long, 10 feet high, and 3 feet deep. It was lovingly named ENIAC, the Electronic Numerical Integrator And Calculator. A true computer with a stored program, it contained about

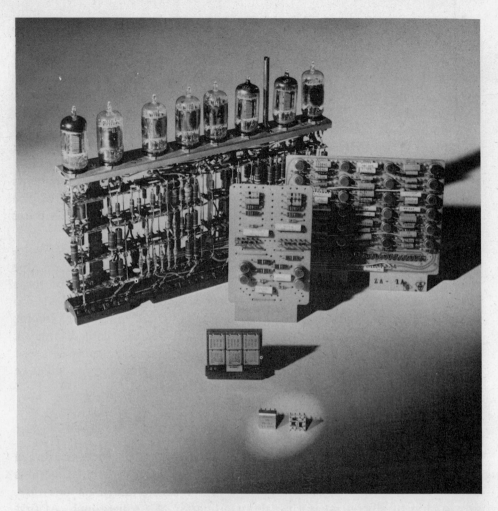

Figure 1. Three generations of computer components. The unit in the background utilized vacuum tubes and discrete components (resistors and diodes). Such units could multiply 2 10-digit numbers 2,000 times per second. Second generation technology is illustrated by the printed circuit cards (center). This technology employed transistors instead of vacuum tubes. They could multiply 2 10-digit numbers 100,000 times per second. Integrated circuits, the third generation of computer technology, illustrated in the center foreground, can multiply 2 10-digit numbers more than 1,000,000 times per second. (Courtesy of IBM)

18,000 tubes (mostly double triodes, for those who know), required 150,000 watts of power, and gave off, as you can imagine, tremendous quantities of heat.

Since this is a book about computers and not politics, I will only say that ENIAC's primary purpose was to calculate trajectories of bombs and shells. Much of its life was spent waiting for its inventors to track down burnt-out tubes. (By way of contrast, I bought a computer in 1978 for

$2 thousand that measures about 18 by 20 by 24 inches, runs on 150 watts, and is to ENIAC what a nuclear reactor is to a campfire.) This was the first generation of computers and it had a very short life. In 1948 both the transistor and I were born and the world hasn't been the same since. This device operated on very small amounts of power and at much higher speeds. It also generated less heat, had a longer life, and was more reliable than the vacuum tube. It quickly replaced vacuum tubes and gave rise to a second generation of computers. (See Figure 1.) The transistors, along with other small, discrete components — capacitors, resistors, diodes, and the like — were mounted on circuit boards. The wires connecting the components were replaced by lines of copper printed on the back of the board. The whole assembly could be easily inserted and pulled out of the computer for servicing.

Finally, in a process understood today by almost no one, these components were shrunk down to dimensions so small that it takes a microscope to see them at all. Anywhere from a dozen to several hundred of these components are deposited onto tiny wafers of silicon and then sealed into ceramic packages, known as integrated circuits. These integrated circuits, lined up like so many centipedes on their circuit boards, enabled fantastic reductions in the size of computers, as well as impressive gains in speed and computational power. This third generation of computers is what we are dealing with today.

THE MICROPROCESSOR REVOLUTION

The complexity of the circuits sealed into these ceramic packages continued to grow. Eventually, the inevitable happened; all of the different functions that make up a full-fledged computer came to be contained on one tiny, square chip of silicon measuring about a quarter of a square inch. At first it required very specialized skills to be able to program these chips to do something useful, and generally, the program given to them at birth never changed again. They were inserted into a product dedicated to one specific task.

Indeed, the world is quickly becoming populated with these microprocessors. They're showing up in obvious places (calculators and electronic games) and not so obvious places (automobile engines, dish and clothes washers, sewing machines, microwave ovens, telephones, television tuning systems, and stereos), and new applications are being developed daily. (See Figure 2.)

THE MICROCOMPUTER REVOLUTION

Microprocessors, as they are described above, are generally given one program that never changes — to run the microwave oven, create different stitches on the sewing machine, tune in the TV signal, etc.

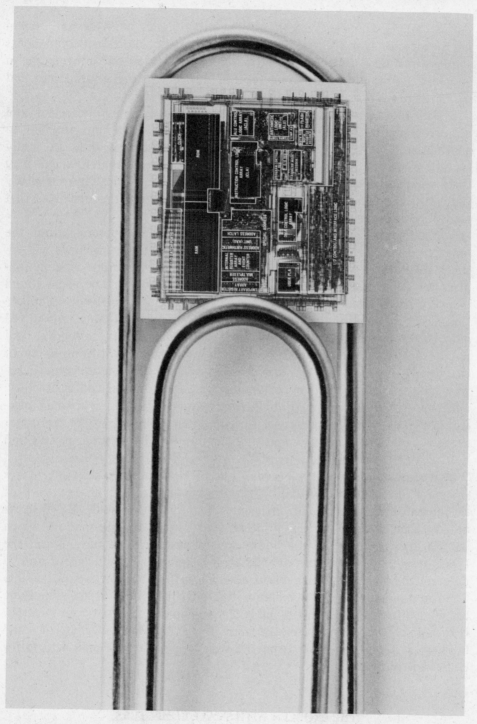

Figure 2. The one-chip computer: offspring of the transistor. The MAC–4 one-chip computer is compared to a standard size paper clip. The chip's numerous functional areas are labeled. (Courtesy of Bell Laboratories)

A microcomputer system, on the other hand, contains not only a microprocessor as the central brain, but also a host of additional components — some memory, a keyboard and a screen display to put information in and read information out, some type of device to store information, and perhaps a printer for hard copies of output.

But the most important distinction between a microprocessor and a microcomputer system is the ability to change from one program to another and the ability to store these programs so that they are easily accessible to the microcomputer system. A microcomputer, then, may be running your accounts receivable one moment, controlling your inventory the next, and later printing mailing labels. These are the machines that we will be concerned with in this book.

Microcomputers have brought the price of computers within the range of a small business. Over the next 25 years these machines will entirely revolutionize our society. Not only will they become as commonplace as calculators in every business, but they will also soon be found in every home. One of the largest effects on society will be to eliminate the need for much of the traveling we do. The advent of large, centralized data bases, microprocessor-controlled communications networks, and microprocessor-based terminal systems in your home will bring many of the things you now travel miles for and spend hours on to your fingertips. You may soon shop by computer for the best prices and availability, bank by computer and pay bills from your telephone, send mail electronically, do your job at home by computer (as many in the computer industry are already doing), and quit commuting. Do more with less and quit wasting the world's resources!

We are standing on the brink of one of humanity's greatest adventures since the invention of writing — the replacement of the drudge work of the human brain by a quiet, efficient, cheap, and tireless device. Because of advances in data storage, printing, and display of information, which will be discussed later in the book, and because of rapid advances in the types of programs available off the shelf (eliminating the need for you to program the machine — also discussed later in the book), it is now possible for you to not only participate in this adventure, but to get something for your efforts that is very tangible and valuable in terms of your business. However, a word of caution. Because of the spanking newness of small business systems, the road from decision to payoff is fraught with difficulties and pitfalls.

THE PROBLEM WITH SMALL COMPUTERS

Can you imagine the development of TV sets without the corresponding development of the TV programming industry? Or a world of beautiful stereo equipment awaiting the development of records and tapes? Or cars without roads? Then how can it be that all across America there are thousands of these small, beautifully elegant, powerful, reliable, and inexpensive computing machines sitting on desks and tabletops with no decent programs to run on them? Believe it or not, it happened — for three reasons.

First, the most recent technological and economical breakthroughs in computers occurred with incredible speed. The perfection of the microprocessor and its myriad specialized applications led to the inevitable creation of a company like MITS of Albuquerque — the first company to provide a low-cost computer in a kit, an elaborate toy for hobbyists.

Second, engineers and entrepreneurs all over the country, seeing the possibilities in mimicking on a small scale what the multimillion-dollar computers were doing on a grand scale, began to put together these fabulous little machines in factories and garages everywhere. They differed from their giant cousins mostly in quantitative ways — they were slower, stored less information, and ran fewer programs. They were also physically smaller and cost a lot less. But qualitatively, they were peers.

In fact, they built so much capability into them, it will be years or decades before these capabilities are fully discovered, let alone exploited. But these people did not know or care about the uses to which the machines were to be put any more than the designer of an automobile cares about where you drive it. The tool was simply delivered to the marketplace.

This lack of marketing insight led to a third problem. If you want to buy a personal or small business computer, just wander into any computer or computer systems dealer store and talk to a sales person. About half of them are engineers who sound like they were reared in a Rand Corporation think tank. Their ability to relate to you in a nontechnical, comprehensible fashion is just about zero. Their other half are sales types whose previous job was pushing stereos, calculators, or shoes. They have the same vocabulary as the engineers, but they don't know what the words mean. In either group, the chances of meeting up with someone who knows anything about your business problems — that is, debits and credits, aged receivables, inventory control, invoicing, etc. — are very slim.

And there is a good reason for this state of affairs. Anybody who has the skills and knowledge to do a good job of selling an automated business system has much better opportunities just about anywhere in the industry. It takes almost as mucy effort to sell a $15 thousand system to an unsophisticated user as it does to sell a $300 thousand system to a large company that has the resources to hire a professional to interface with the sales agent. At 10% commission, what is going to attract that sales agent to work in a computer store? Nothing.

Now, add to this lack of sales expertise the fact that there are almost no decent programs available to sell with the computer and you've got a real mess on your hands. In short, the quality of the business software in the software jungle is as poor as the quality of the hardware is good. Why? Well, either the programs were written by a business person, in which case it incorporates all the correct accounting principles in a system that operates with the grace and ease of a three-legged St. Bernard, or they were written by a computer whiz with no business experience, in which case its elegance and operational simplicity are overshadowed only by its inability to do the job completely and correctly.

As owner and operator of a small business, you know that the only way to get something done right is to do it yourself. The project of bringing a small computer into your business is no exception. Since there is no one willing to tell you how to get this particular job done, you're going to have to educate yourself.

This does not require becoming a crack programmer or an electronics technician. The remaining chapters of this book are designed to prepare you for a successful trip to the computer store, to give you the requisite background to evaluate the programs you'll need to buy, and to show you how computer systems work (not just the buttons to push or the programs to run, but also the manual support your system will require). In short, it should educate you to the point where you can successfully integrate an automated system into your business.

MYTHS DEBUNKED

Before proceeding into the mysteries of the hardware, I think I had better unburden you of a few of the more popular myths about computers that most people have.

(1) "My computer will pay for itself." Depending on the conditions in your business, this may or may not be initially true. Whatever the size of your business now, given the same level of activity, a computer will probably cost more than it will return, unless it eliminates some excessive expenses in the general and administrative category or helps you to track down sources of inventory shrinkage. Remember, in addition to the cost of hardware and software (the programs), there will always be some maintenance and repair costs and the time spent fussing with the system and keying information into your data files.

Lest these warnings seem overly pessimistic, let me assure you that the chances of your system eventually paying for itself are excellent. But the payoff will most likely come as your business expands. The computer should be regarded as a tool for growth. If your current methods are marginally adequate for the level of activity in your business now, how will they fare as the business activity escalates? Will the index card inventory system work for you when the number of items in inventory doubles?

How many outstanding receivables can you tolerate before a timely aged accounts receivable report becomes necessary to maintain a healthy cash flow?

There are also intangible benefits to be realized from computerizing. Although a specific dollar amount cannot be assigned to these benefits, they should be considered in the cost/benefit decision process. Chief among these is the peace of mind and increased productivity that comes from an orderly and well-controlled business. Another area is opportunity costs. Stockouts in finished goods can lead to lost sales; lack of order and discipline in the accounts payable department can irritate vendors and result in loss of suppliers; faulty or missing sales history information can lead to bad decisions on whether to grant credit. The latter can lead to bad debts or offended customers.

If your business is small and you know all the customers by their first names, this may not be a big problem. But what happens when the customer list grows from 20 to 200 and this task is delegated to a paid employee? Policies for this decision-making process will have to be devised, with accurate and complete data made available to carry them out.

(2) "Computers are terribly smart. I'll just crank up some programs and let it make all my decisions for me." In fact, computers are terribly dumb. They can add and subtract at the speed of light. They can even do multiplication and division by successive addition and subtraction. They can also make a yes/no type of decision of the most rudimentary type, based on one isolated bit of information. (And it's your responsibility to see that this bit of information contains the correct value.) But that's all. Of course, by stringing together lots of additions, subtractions, and itty-bitty decisions, we can give the computer the appearance of doing something very complex and sophisticated. Nevertheless, it still remains as dumb and faithful to your instructions as ever.

For a thrilling example of how things can go wrong with a computer program, look at Figure 3. This shows what the computer is instructed to do about inventory control on a certain item. Every time you reach 10 units on hand, you want to order 1,000 more. But you have mistakenly told the computer to order 100,000. A clerk might question the size of the order, but a computer will blithely bankrupt you at the speed of light, which is why they say in the data processing industry, "Garbage-in, garbage-out."

Incidentally, you have just read what may have been your first flow chart. Easy, wasn't it? You simply read what's in the boxes and follow the arrows from one process to the next. Flowcharting is one of the most valuable tools available to the programmer to organize the flow of instructions and information through a program. Systems analysts also use flowcharts on a higher level to diagram the operation of complex systems.

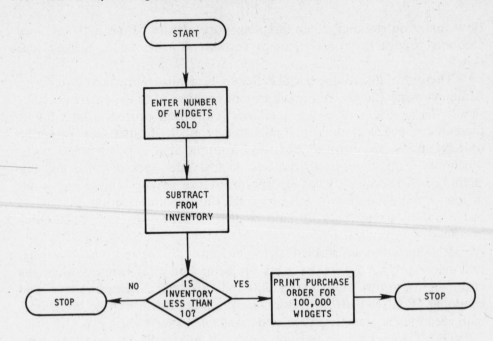

Figure 3.   A simple flowchart.

I have found that flowcharts work just as well on noncomputer problems. It's a great way to organize your thoughts, and it can graphically point out where the holes or weak spots are in a process or procedure you are trying to design for your business.

Many different types of flowcharting symbols have become conventional in the industry and most of them need not concern us here. However, allow me to introduce just one more which is instrumental to all tasks given to computers — the decision symbol:

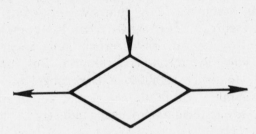

The status of some piece of data written inside the symbol is evaluated, and one of two (or sometimes three) paths are taken out of the diamond to different processes in the flowchart. (See Figure 4.)

Note the "feedback loop" (the line from "Go to sleep for an hour" to "Wake up"). Looping in a repetitive process is one of the things that computers do best and humans do worst. Note that in the loop shown, you cannot get out of the loop (or bed) until it stops raining. If Noah

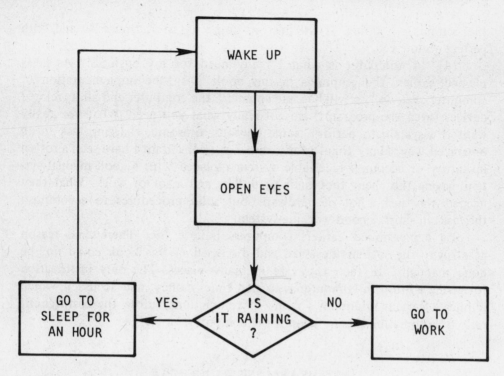

Figure 4. The feedback loop; Noah's dilemma.

had used this program, all the animals might have starved. At best he'd have had a terrible mess to clean up.

For more information on flowcharting symbols, see Appendix G.

(3) "Computers are beyond my understanding. I don't know much math. I'll have to hire someone expensive to tend it." Wrong on all counts. First, there is nothing beyond your understanding going on in that computer that you have to know. By the time you've finished this book you'll be amazed at how simple and accessible computer systems actually are. Of course, you won't be able to fix the system if the hardware malfunctions and you may not be able to fix bugs in your purchased programs (not your responsibility, anyway), but then, you don't repair your typewriter, copier, car, or TV, do you?

As for programming, that too is easy. Golf is harder. Tennis is harder. Getting to work on Monday is harder. Once a problem is properly analyzed and a solution is mapped out, programming becomes an almost mechanical task: just like hitting a softball.

Computers imitate life. How much math do you really use in your business — linear regression or standard deviation? Probably, you never get past percentages. Since your computer is going to help you with your current problems, you are going to have it do just what you do now or would like to do but can't for lack of time. You'll understand everything the computer is doing. It will just be doing it faster, tirelessly, and with perfect accuracy.

(4) "A computer is what I really need for my business." As I explained earlier, the emphasis in this book is on the implementation of computer *systems.* As will become apparent, the computer and all its related devices (even the programs) are not really what you need. What you really want is a system to perform some onerous, tiresome, exacting task in an organized way. Many times in my career as a consultant I have seen a rotten inventory or accounts receivable system replaced with a good manual system, saving the client thousands of dollars and a lot of work. What they needed was not a lot of hardware, but solid procedures to accomplish the task: in short, a good working system.

As I mentioned earlier, computers imitate life. There's no reason at all why the systems designed and discussed in this book could not be done manually. In fact, they are in many places. The only justification for giving a job to a computer is to gain time, money, and accuracy, which implies a certain minimum volume of transactions before the cost/benefit ratio of automating tilts in favor of the computer.

SYSTEMS ANALYSIS MADE SIMPLE

Most people have heard of systems analysts, although I'm sure very few people know exactly what one does. Before a computer program is written, someone has to sit down with the user or customer and talk about information requirements. This is the job of the systems analyst, who then translates the requirements into specifications that a programmer can understand. Once the customer approves the specifications, the programming begins. These specifications include items like the format of reports that will be printed, the kinds of information to be put into the program, and the format and content of any information to be stored in the computer.

As you can imagine, this job requires some special skills, since the systems analyst needs to know both the language of the user and the language of the computer. However, there is a very simple way of looking at the whole job of systems analysis. It really boils down to the answers to four questions:

1. Input — What are the inputs to this system?
2. Process — What processes go on inside this system?
3. Output — What are the outputs of this system?
4. Storage — What information is stored by this system for later retrieval?

The way this looks in flowchart form is shown in Figure 5.

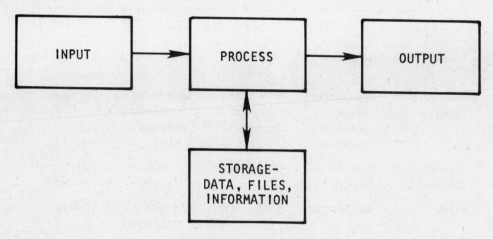

Figure 5. The primal system.

No matter how complex the system, it can always be reduced to these four functions. Of course, there is no reason why this technique of analysis has to be confined to computer systems. Any activity in life can be broken down into a system with these four functions. Some examples are given in Figure 6.

These four functions are what I like to call the *primal system*, and I will be referring back to them throughout the book. It is a good way to get a handle on any complex problem whether or not it relates to a computer. Since you have probably been using this technique unconsciously for many of your own problems, you are already a systems analyst.

Now, let us regard the functions of a computer system using the primal system approach to see if we can't shed a little more light on what advantages a computer will bring you.

1. *Storage* — All data are in one location, readily available to you through a program rather than scattered in files all over the office. A customer calls in an order for a thousand widgets. You put him or her on hold and turn to the terminal on your desk. How many are in stock? Check the inventory file. How many are on order? Check the open purchase order file for quantity and date of shipment. Is the customer's credit good? Look at the accounts receivable file. These kinds of instant answers enable you to make decisions based on facts.
2. *Input* — The computer will organize your data at the source, check for accuracy, control the flow, and centralize the activity.
3. *Process* — The biggest advantage here is speed and accuracy. The next plus that you'll probably discover is that you are able to do things that were impractical manually. How about checking your complete inventory every day? Or every hour? How about

SYSTEM	INPUT	STORAGE	PROCESS	OUTPUT
Toothbrushing	Dirty teeth	Toothpaste, toothbrush	Brush 'em	Clean teeth
Investment analysis	Stockbroker's advice, economic conditions	Price history, financial statements	Criteria for judgement of data and inputs	Decision
Manufacture of widgets	Order for 10 widgets	Widget pieces	Assembly of widgets	Ten complete widgets
Family	Man, woman, love, sex	Clergy, city hall	Marriage procreation	Children

Figure 6. Some real life examples of the primal system.

knowing which customers provided what percentage of sales this month? How about an up-to-date aged accounts receivable on demand? Before a sales trip, wouldn't it be nice to know what customers average more than $10 thousand per month in the Pacific Northwest?

4. *Output* — The reports you generate, either printed or displayed on a terminal, will be error-free (assuming your inputs are not garbage), legible, complete, and timely. You will also be inventing new reports impractical to generate manually, which will give you new ways of looking at your business.

In the next chapter I will use the primal system approach to introduce to you the various components of the microcomputer system. Although I will repeatedly stress the importance of the programs over the hardware, I think it will be much easier for you to understand the applications presented in Chapter 5 after some of your curiosity about these marvelous electronic and mechanical devices has been satisfied. Therefore, on with the show.

2

HARDWARE

INTRODUCTION

It would be nice if you could buy a computer the way you buy a blender — with everything in one box. You just unpack it, plug it in, and it runs. You don't even have to read the directions, do you? Well, microcomputer systems are moving in that direction; it's called the *turnkey* approach. This is a sort of archaic (already) phrase that refers to a significant aesthetic revolution in computer systems.

It used to be that the hallmark of every computer was a bank or two of rapidly blinking lights and a flock of switches with esoteric labels on them. As the market expanded to include people who wanted to use their computers for business applications, instead of for scientific work or advanced industrial research and development, the number of lights and switches diminished to the point that the user hardly ever needed to touch a switch and certainly never to read (or even know *how* to read) the lights on the front of the box. So the lights and switches were eliminated entirely and replaced by a conventional lock and key. To turn the computer on, you simply insert the key in the lock and turn it. Like magic, the computer starts running your programs.

Today, even systems that don't have keys (those that start up and run without the user having to play with the switches) are called turnkey. So now, to add to your confusion, there are two ways to buy your hardware. One is to purchase a turnkey package with all the hardware and programs together. This can be from a vendor who probably buys large amounts of hardware from a manufacturer at a steep discount, adds some programs written for a particular market segment — like lawyers (word processing and timekeeping), doctors (medical billings). and construction (job costing) — and sells the whole thing for a package price. The second way, which we call the adventurous method, is to stroll into a computer store and shop for the components and programs yourself.

15

Either way, you'll have to know something about hardware. You'll have to select among lots of options and you'll have to know what each of the components does. You should know what to expect from them and what their limits are. Fortunately, we have a very neat method of describing this information to you in the form of the primal system that was explained in Chapter 1. As you remember, a computer system, like every other system in creation, does just four things: takes in information (input), manipulates it in some way (process), keeps it in an organized way for later use (storage), and shows the results of its handiwork (output). There are pieces of hardware designed to perform each of these tasks. Hooking them all together in the right combination will yield you a functioning computer system.

In this chapter I will describe the principle types of components you'll need to know about and how they fulfill one (or in some cases, two) of the four basic system functions.

INPUT DEVICES

There is only one practical way to get information into your system, and that is through the keyboard, a device that looks like a typewriter keyboard. (See Figure 7.) This keyboard might also have a 10-key pad, similar to a calculator keypad, to the right of the alphabetic keys. This pad facilitates the entry of numeric data — a very desirable feature. There will also be a few extra keys with strange words on them, like "break" and "clear." The "break" key does not break the machine. The "clear" key will not clear up your confusion. Read on.

There is almost no functional difference among computer keyboards. They're all laid out more or less the same way, like a typewriter. However, there are great differences in quality, reflected mostly in the "feel" of the keys as you depress them. Some work smoothly and quietly, some are hard to press, and some depress too easily. Some will make a click or pop when they are depressed, which gives a nice positive feel to the board. (If you've ever switched from a calculator that gives no tactile response to one that clicks when it is pressed, you know what I mean.) Preferences are entirely a personal matter. Your ideal keyboard can be found only through use. You will get plenty of experience on them if you follow my plan for buying software in Chapter 4.

There are a couple of terms you should know with regard to keyboards. Sales literature will refer to "upper and lower case." Some keyboards will generate only upper case or capital letters. Others will allow you to type both capital and small (lower case) letters. The latter is generally more desirable. The literature will also talk about a "full ASCII character set." ASCII, the American Standard Code for Information Interchange, is a

Figure 7. A keyboard shown without case. (Courtesy of HI-TEK, Inc.)

convention adopted by most computer manufacturers that makes their equipment and programs compatible with the equipment and programs of other manufacturers. The "code" refers to the way the characters keyed by you on the keyboard are stored inside the computer. The only other popular standard is EBCDIC, the Extended Binary Coded Decimal Interchange Code, found mostly in IBM machines.

There are several ways that other larger systems input their data. They involve very complex pieces of machinery that, in addition to being several times larger and several times more expensive than my whole personal computer system, do not have much application on microprocessor-based systems. Optical character recognition (OCR) machines "read" characters by their shape. Card readers read the familiar punched cards at speeds that you would not believe. The characters at the bottom of your bank checks are printed in magnetic ink that can be read by machines.

Looking down the electronic road a few years, one can see voice input devices becoming a reality. This is a device into which you would be able to speak a variety of commands, instructions, and numbers. The device would then present this data to the computer as if it came from the keyboard. The advantages are obvious — greater speed of input and reduction of transcription errors. The problems to be overcome, however, are formidable. Chief among these is how to get a computer to recognize a word like "four" spoken by a Southerner, a New Yorker, a slight person with a wispy voice, a dock foreman, Truman Capote, George C. Scott, and Mae West.

For the nonce though, since keyboards are the only practical way to get information into the computer, be sure to get one of these when you buy your system.

OUTPUT DEVICES

There are only two ways to get information out of your computer. The first is the CRT or cathode ray tube. These are the TV screens you always see computer operators peering into so intently. When CRTs come attached to a keyboard, the whole assembly is referred to as a terminal. As you can tell by now, a terminal is an indispensible item in a computer system. As you type on the keyboard, each character depressed is displayed (or "echoed," as they say) on the CRT. This is handy because you can see right away if you have made any mistakes. The more common use of the CRT is to display small quantities of information like the quantity on hand of a certain inventory item or a sales order.

The only problem with these CRTs is that they "scroll," that is, as a new line of information appears at the bottom of the screen, all the information moves up one line and the top line rolls off the screen and disappears. If you want to see it again, you have to have the computer redisplay it.

The other principal way to get information out of your computer is to print it. Printers for microprocessors are undergoing rapid evolution. Over the last 2 or 3 years the quality of the printing has improved, the speed has been greatly increased, and reliability has become much better — all while prices have remained the same or even dropped. And by the time this book has been out for a year or two, the prices will be even lower (despite inflation) and the performances even better.

When information is printed on a printer, as opposed to being displayed on the screen of a terminal, it is referred to as "hard copy." A hard-copy device of some kind is indispensable to a business application. If you are going to explore automation by taking the low buck route, you will be a little put off by having to spend more for your printer than for the main computer itself. But didn't you spend more for your stereo speakers than for your amplifier? The printer is a precision device. It has to make dozens of individual movements every second, and in such a way that the letters produced will look straight and legible even upon close examination. Take some time out at the computer store to find out how they work and you'll be amazed. The price of having your own printing press will begin to look very cheap. Thinking over the history of the printed word and its value to civilization will give you an appreciation for the enormous revolution through which you are living right now. Gutenberg would have been pleased.

There are two basic types of printers: the line printer and the character printer. Line printers are fast and expensive. As the information streams out to the printer, the line printer cleverly stores up information until it has a whole line's worth. Then, in an instant, the whole line is printed. In this way, speeds of 400 to 600 lines per minute are common; 4,000 to 6,000 lines per minute are not unheard of, although such a lot of output in a short time can rarely be expected on what we are defining as a small business system.

A more prosaic approach is taken by the character printer, which sensibly prints one character at a time, although it can print quickly enough — typically from 60 to 600 characters per second. Some print only from left to right, then return to start another line at the left margin. Some of them, however, are bi-directional; that is, when the printing mechanism reaches the right-hand margin, it waits until the computer has sent another complete line of information, then prints it in reverse from right to left. Since the speed at which the carriage returns from right to left is usually about the same as its printing speed from left to right, printing in both directions can double the lines per minute printed with only a small additional cost. Bidirectional printing is a very attractive feature in serial printers.

CHARACTER SETS

!"#$%&'()*+,-./0123456789:;<=>?

@ABCDEFGHIJKLMNOPQRSTUVWXYZ[\]^_

`abcdefghijklmnopqrstuvwxyz{|}~

!"#$%&'()*+,-./0123456789:;<=>?

@ABCDEFGHIJKLMNOPQRSTUVW
XYZ[\]^_

`abcdefghijklmnopqrstuvwxyz{|}~

!"#$%&'()*+,-./0123456789:;<=>?

@ABCDEFGHIJKLMNOPQRSTUVWXYZ[\]^_

`abcdefghijklmnopqrstuvwxyz{|}^

!"#$%&'()*+,-./01234567
89:;<=>?

@ABCDEFGHIJKLMNOPQRSTUVW
XYZ[\]^_

`abcdefghijklmnopqrstuvw
xyz{|}^

!"#$%&'()*+,-./0123456789:;<=>?

@ABCDEFGHIJKLMNOPQRSTUVWXYZ[\]^_

`abcdefghijklmnopqrstuvwxyz{|}^

!"#$%&'()*+,-./0123456789:;<=>?

@ABCDEFGHIJKLMNOPQRSTUVWXYZ[\]^_

`abcdefghijklmnopqrstuvwxyz{|}^

Figure 8.   An example of dot matrix printing.

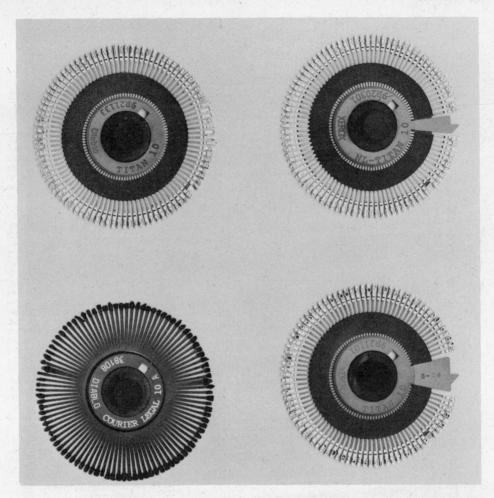

Figure 9. Daisy wheel print mechanisms. (Diablo and Xerox are registered trademarks of Xerox Corporation. Photos furnished courtesy of Diablo Systems, Inc., a Xerox Company)

The other factor to consider when choosing your printer is the purpose for which your output will be used. You see, there are two popular ways to print a character. One is the dot matrix method, so called because each letter is formed out of a matrix or grid of dots. The greater the number of dots in the matrix, the better the quality of the letters formed. The most common matrix is 5 dots wide and 7 dots high. From these 35 dots, believe it or not, a very legible set of characters can be formed — not just capitals, but lower case, numbers, punctuation marks, and a variety of special characters, as well. (See Figure 8.) However, compared to the beauty

Artisan Legal 12

ABCDEFGHIJKLMNOPQRSTUVWXYZabcdefghijklmnopqrstuvwxyz
0123456789   ½¢,.:;-+$#%¤¶[]()†=§"°©!?!@*/ ̄®¾/ "¡¿"

Forms Gothic S-10

ABCDEFGHIJKLMNOPQRSTUVWXYZabcdefghijklmnopqrstuvwxyz
0123456789   ¬¢,.:;-+$#%{}[]()>=<`'`?!@*/|\&" ̄_

ABCDEFGHIJKLMNOPQRSTUVWXYZabcdefghijklmnopqrstuvwxyz
0123456789   ¬¢,.:;-+$#%{}[]()>=<¤'b◇?!:%/|\&" ̄_

Manifold 10

Dual Gothic Legal 12

ABCDEFGHIJKLMNOPQRSTUVWXYZabcdefghijklmnopqrstuvwxyz
0123456789   ½¢,.:;-+$#%¤¶[]()†=§"°©!?!@*/ ̄®&" ̄_

OCR-A 10

ABCDEFGHIJKLMNOPQRSTUVWXYZabcdefghijklmnopqrstuvwxyz
0123456789   ¥Ñ,.:;-+$£%ÄÜÆ{}H=⌐,'|.?|╀*/Ö∅&"

OCR-B 10

ABCDEFGHIJKLMNOPQRSTUVWXYZabcdefghijklmnopqrstuvwxyz
0123456789   ¤£,.:;-+$#%{}[]()>=<`'`.'?!@*/|\&" ̄_

OCR-B 10 Scandia

ABCDEFGHIJKLMNOPQRSTUVWXYZabcdefghijklmnopqrstuvwxyz
0123456789   ,.:;-+¤#%äåäÅÅ()>=<üʼÜé?!€*/öö&" ̄_

APL-10

α⊥∩⌊∈ ∇∆⍳∘'⌷□|⊤∘∗?ρ⌈~↓⍵⊃⊢⊂ABCDEFGHIJKLMNOPQRSTUVWXYZ
0123456789 ¯•‥⍪([+÷≤←={}↑→∨∧:×;$]≥◊'¨¯≠/→⊢>)-

French Prestige Cubic 10

ABCDEFGHIJKLMNOPQRSTUVWXYZabcdefghijklmnopqrstuvwxyz
0123456789 |Ⴑ,.:;-+$£%éè°§()>=<¨'·?ià∗/ùç&"_

Russian Cubic 10

АБЦДЕФГЧИЖКЛМНОПЩРСТУВШХЫЗабцдефѓчижжклмнопшрстувшхыз
0123456789 Ъ',.:Э-+Ю#%Йю[]==<()]_|ЫЯзэ¨ч|ъ¦_

Kana Gothic Elite 12

ABCDEFGHIJKLMNOPQRSTUVW#YZ クヨウテニモカナコヌリシツコトホワチオリンムイ٢I
ラ〳タ_ハ٢リ"2٤١セ-ヒメフ٣,0.ル+)(@/98765*Χマネネスサミ٤ロ゜ル

Kana Gothic Pica 10

ABCDEFGHIJKLMNOPQRSTUVW#YZ クヨウテニモカナコヌリシツコトホワチオリンムイ٢I
+)(@/98765 ^ヌ,.*X0٣٤21オメ٣ニ□トメメネⴹ=-ノルスハサフルラ٢ピゼ゜

Figure 10. Examples of different type faces available on impact printers (Courtesy of Diablo Systems, Inc., a Xerox Company)

23

of the typewritten page, they leave a lot to be desired. They look like they came out of a computer. In fact, they're downright ugly. But if the information you need printed is going to be used for purely internal purposes, what's the difference? Even a dot matrix purchase or sales order is very acceptable in today's business environment.

However, if you want something that looks like it was typewritten, and your primary application is to produce letters and other documents for public consumption, then impact printers are for you. These are printers equipped with small wheels that have many spokes. On the end of each spoke is a letter. The wheel spins with the ribbon and paper on one side and a hammer on the other. As the spoke with the letter to be printed comes around, the hammer jumps out and smacks the letter against the ribbon, producing an impression on the paper. (See Figure 9.)

The entire complement of upper and lower case, numeric, and punctuation characters is on the wheel (sometimes called a "daisy" wheel). The print quality is as fine as any ever produced. However, there are two drawbacks to this method. The first is that this type of printer is much more expensive than a dot matrix printer. You must be prepared to spend from 50% to 100% more for the impact printer than the dot matrix printer. The second is that the print speed is much slower; it is something on the order of 40 to 60 characters per second. So, if appearance isn't a problem, dot matrix is the way to go. However, if word processing is your bag, get the impact printer. Most manufacturers provide a variety of easily changed wheels with different type faces. (See Figure 10 for examples of different type faces available on impact printers.)

Reliability and high quality are critical factors in the selection of a printer. These are electromechanical devices, and as such are subject to vibration and wear. A manufacturer with a track record of good quality control, a reputation for well-engineered products, and readily available service is much to be preferred. There will always be cheap printers on the market, put out by new companies trying to make inroads into the established market. Some of these cheap "miracles" turn out to be good machines, but generally you get what you pay for.

Almost all manufacturers of computer equipment warrant their products for 90 days. After that you're on your own. And service, not to mention freight charges to and from the service center, is very expensive. Be sure to find out from the sales person just where the nearest service center for your printer is and how much is charged for service. Nothing is more irritating to an active computer user, particularly in a small business environment, than to suffer printer withdrawal. If the computer store services equipment on the spot, find out if the servicers have had training at the manufacturer's plant and are recognized by the manufacturer as qualified.

PROCESSORS

It's getting harder and harder to find a computer anymore. (What is he talking about? I thought there were supposed to be more of them than ever.) Yes, there are more computers, but they're not as visible as they used to be. Drop into a Radio Shack store somewhere and look at one of their computer systems. You'll se the CRT, keyboard, printer, and some other mysterious boxes, but where is the computer itself? Believe it or not, it's in the space under the keyboard or possibly inside the cabinet with the CRT.

It's no wonder then that evaluating the processor part of a whole computer system can be so confusing and difficult. There isn't even a box to point to anymore; no blinking lights, no switches. Fortunately there is not very much you need to know about processors. Even though they come in more varieties than white wine, the biggest differences among them are due to the software or programs that they run and not the actual hardware itself.

There are some people who will tell you that this is not true, that the processor is the most important part of the system, and that you should understand it. Chances are the person telling you this understands the esoteric machinations of the microcircuitry and will immediately proceed to impress — and confuse — you immensely. Unfortunately, chances are that this person is also trying to sell you a computer, not a business system. (Are you beginning to get a sense of the difference between a computer and a whole system?)

I once bought a fairly high performance car. I didn't then, and I do not now, know how many carburetors the engine had, what the cubic inches of displacement were, or anything about the bore, the stroke, or the dwell. I retained all this ignorance in spite of the fact that the engine is the heart of the automotive system. Nevertheless, the car went faster than I needed it to and I didn't have any trouble driving it.

But just to show you how irrelevant many of the specifications of processors that will be touted to you are, here are some of the things with which you can engage a salesperson in conversation.

The chip. The microprocessor chip is where the actual work of the computer is done. (See Figure 11.) It contains the circuitry to do the arithmetic operations, to compare one piece of data to another, to fetch data from the memory and store it back, etc. In the spirit of the technological revolution, they have numbers, not names. Chances are the system you buy will have in it either a Z80, 8080 or 8080A, 6502, or 6800. They're made by companies like Mostek, Texas Instruments, Motorola, and Fairchild. Now when the sales person asks you "Do you want a Z80- or 6800-

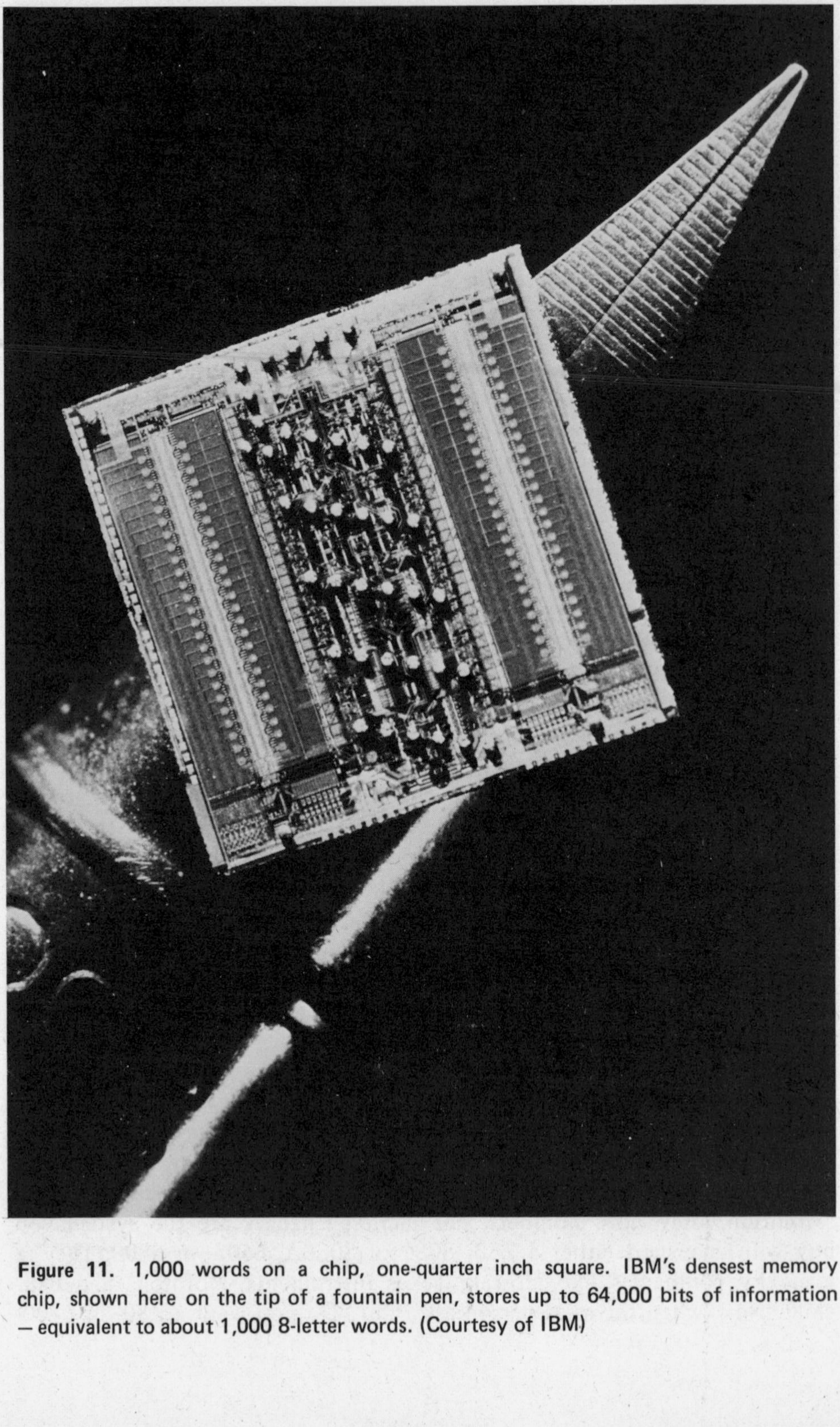

Figure 11. 1,000 words on a chip, one-quarter inch square. IBM's densest memory chip, shown here on the tip of a fountain pen, stores up to 64,000 bits of information — equivalent to about 1,000 8-letter words. (Courtesy of IBM)

based system?" you can glibly reply, "I don't care. What kind of software support do you offer?"

Speed. Some computers operate faster than others. The speed is measured in cycle time, clock speed in hertz, time required to add two 10-digit numbers, and even more arcane measurements. It is difficult to relate these figures to the real world. (Use these figures for comparison only. Your actual speed may vary.) There are many factors other than processor speed that will affect how fast your aged receivables report comes off the printer. One processor that is twice as fast as another many actually produce a report slower due to inefficiencies in programming, slower data transfer rates, or a clumsy operating system (defined later).

Memory. Memory is where the programs (which contain the instructions to be executed by the computer) and the data (on which the programs operate) are stored. Memory is measured by the "K," which comes from the Greek word kilo, meaning 1,000. Actually, one K of memory is 1,024, which is a nice round number in the binary or base-two numbering system used by all computers (2 to the tenth power for you mathematicians out there).

But, you might be asking, 1,024 what? The answer is 1,024 bytes. I will temporarily define a byte as equivalent to one character, letter, or number. If there are 2,182 letters, spaces, and punctuation marks on this page, then it would take 2,182 bytes to store this page in the memory. The idea of bytes is explained further in another section. Just remember, the more memory you have in your system, the more information you can work on at one time and the bigger the programs you can run. 8K is the minimum requirement to get started. This is really limited and in practice there are no business systems I know of running on 8K. 64K generally gives you all the flexibility you need and is a more or less standard amount of memory for a small business system.

If you take the turnkey approach to buying a system, you'll be provided with a certain amount of memory that will be sufficient to do the job. If you're taking the adventurous approach, the questions you'll want answered are: (1) How much memory do I need to run the software I'm considering? (2) What is the maximum amount of memory this machine will accept? (3) Can this maximum amount of memory fit inside the main computer enclosure? (4) Or is an expansion chassis available in case I exceed the limits of this machine's chassis? (5) What is the cost and availability of memory? Remember that the processor price quoted generally includes little or no memory, and you must have memory to run the system.

RAM, ROM, and CORE. There are three words you will often hear in reference to memories while shopping for a computer: RAM, ROM, and CORE. All three refer to types of memory.

RAM is an acronym which stands for Random Access Memory. It is made from semiconductors and packaged into chips in much the same way as the microprocessor. The contents of the memory can be changed at will. Memory is where the data and the programs that operate on them are located. Information displayed on the CRT or printer comes from RAM. Information keyed in through the keyboard goes into RAM. When someone says "This system has 32K of memory," it is the 32 × 1,024 bytes of random access memory they are talking about.

ROM stands for Read Only Memory. It is very similar to RAM except that, as the name implies, information can only be read out. Nothing can be written into ROM. In microcomputers the ROM contains special programming given to it at the factory. This program never changes. It is responsible for helping the computer to run other programs that are stored in RAM.

CORE is an obsolete word referring to an ancient (over 20 years old — how does that make you feel?) method of memory storage. COREs are little doughnut-shaped rings of ferrite with wires threaded through them. (They are about the size of the period at the end of this sentence.) The current flowing through the wires magnetizes the COREs in one direction or the other to represent bits of information. CORE memory is still being used on some large machines, but even there it is being replaced by semiconductor memory (RAM) in the newer models. CORE memory is extremely more expensive to build and service than semiconductor memory and therefore is rarely, if ever, used in microcomputers.

Number of input/output ports. The place where a support device such as a CRT or keyboard is plugged in is called a port. It is important that your machine have enough ports to plug in all of the devices you want to hook to the computer now or in the future. Once again, a good analogy is the home stereo. On the back of a stereo are jacks ("ports") to plug in input (phonograph, tape, or tuner) and output (speakers or tape) devices. If you buy a unit that allows only your reel-to-reel tape to be plugged in and later buy a cassette deck, you're out of luck, aren't you? You have to buy a different unit. Since the number of places available on a computer to plug in other kinds of input and output devices is fixed, be sure to determine whether or not they will be adequate for your present and future needs. You'll be glad you did.

Software support. This is one area that is difficult to simplify. You will need to understand what these items do before deciding what you need. Since the advent of small business systems has been so recent and is changing so rapidly, software support is generally weak compared to that available on older, larger machines. For a more detailed discussion, see Chapter 3. For now, suffice it to say that good (meaning bug-free, efficient programming that does the required job) manufacturer-supplied software is worth its weight in gold. It will save hours of programming time needed to develop your own software and it will provide you with design features which, unless you are experienced in systems design, you would probably not discover yourself.

Instruction set. At its most fundamental level, a computer can do a limited number of things. It can for instance add, subtract, multiply, divide, compare two numbers, accept information from the outside world (through one of its ports), send information out, and perform a variety of other more technical tasks. Each of these activities is triggered by the execution of one of these instructions. The more instructions a machine can execute, the more powerful and flexible it is. Taken as a group, these instructions are referred to as the "instruction set." The term "command" is often used interchangeably with "instruction."

Unless you are a programmer, it will be difficult to evaluate a computer's instruction set. Fortunately, there are only a few things you need to be aware of regarding your machine's instruction set. Hardware-implemented multiply and divide instructions will give you a faster execution time for arithmetic operations than a machine that does these operations by successive addition and subtraction. Floating point instructions (sometimes available as an option) will make statistical and scientific applications easier to implement and will make your business applications run faster. Otherwise the program needs to keep track of the decimal point, which takes time and memory. However, for commercial applications the floating decimal point (depending on how the program is written) can sometimes lead to rounding errors, which may be intolerable in your environment.

STORAGE DEVICES

Storage devices are used by the computer as both input and output devices. That is, the computer gets the information and the programs it needs from the storage device and saves data and programs on them. The two operations are referred to as "read" and "write." Storage devices fall into two broad categories, which refer to the way information is stored on and retrieved from them.

Serial devices. The first type, serial storage, is done on magnetic tape, most commonly in the form of a cassette identical to the ones used for audio recording. It's called serial because in order to get to information in the middle of the tape, it is necessary to read each record on the tape from the beginning until the required record is found. The next step up from cassette — which is slow, cheap, and unreliable — is the large, expensive tape drives, which are generally not supported on small systems and are very costly. Cassettes are pretty much the personal computer/ hobbyist tool now and have very little place in the small business environment.

There is another serial access device that is on the rise, and that is the tape cartridge drive. Tape cartridge drives have come onto the market recently to solve the backup problem posed by a new kind of disk drive — the Winchester — which I will describe later in more detail. Tape cartridge drives have very high transfer rates; that is, they can accept data from and feed data to the computer at very high speeds. They are reliable and each tape cartridge holds a lot of data. They are used mostly for making copies of data files and for archiving large amounts of data not needed on-line.

When a device is on-line, it is connected directly to the computer and is available to receive information from the computer or to send information to the computer. The opposite condition is, obviously enough, "off-line." These terms can be applied to data stored on a tape as well. If your cassette deck is hooked to your computer it is "on-line." Now, if you take 1 of 10 recorded tapes, place it in the cassette, and make it ready to be read by the computer, that tape and that information or data is "on-line." The information on the other 9 tapes is "off-line."

As an on-line data storage and retrieval device, tape has very limited usefulness.

Random devices. The other access method is random access. This implies that any piece of data on the device can be accessed without reading through all of the information on the device to find the required record. The most popular small systems random access device is the diskette or flexible disk, or floppy disk — so called because the storage medium is made of a sheet of flexible material packaged in a nonrigid envelope. The diskette, which looks like nothing so much as a 45–RPM record, comes in two sizes: a 5½" diameter (known as mini-floppy) and an 8" diameter size. The mini-floppies hold about 90 kilobytes (characters) of information each, and the standard floppies hold about 256 kilobytes each.

The device that reads the information on a diskette and sends it to the computer and takes information from the computer and writes it onto the diskette is known as a "drive."

When you insert a diskette into its drive and shut the door, the diskette begins to spin and a read/write head similar to the recording head on a tape deck touches down on the recording surface such that the path the head makes on the diskette is a circle or "track." The head can be moved along the radius of the diskette so that any number of tracks can be read and

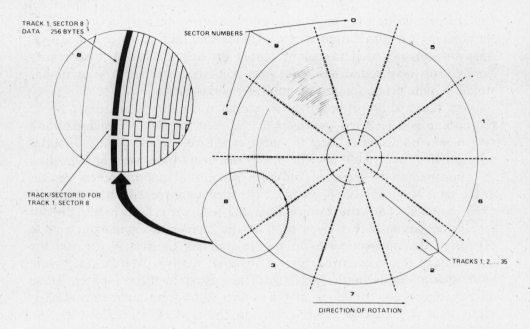

TRACK 1, SECTOR 8
DATA   256 BYTES

SECTOR NUMBERS

TRACK/SECTOR ID FOR
TRACK 1, SECTOR 8

TRACKS 1, 2, ... 35

DIRECTION OF ROTATION

Figure 12. Track/sector organization on a formatted diskette. (Courtesy of Radio Shack, a division of Tandy Corp. © Tandy Corp. Fort Worth, TX)

written on the diskette. Of course, a minimum amount of space must be left between the tracks to keep the information from overlapping. A certain amount of space must separate each bit of information along a track as well. These two distances put a limit on the maximum amount of information that can be stored on one diskette. By moving the head in and out along the radius of the diskette, any point on the diskette can be accessed; hence, random access.

Each track is further divided into 8, 10, or 16 "sectors," marked off by radii. (See Figure 12.) This sector most commonly holds either 128 or 256 bytes, or characters of information. Information is generally transferred between disk and computer a sector at a time.

There are a couple of specifications you can use to compare drives. One is the speed of rotation — higher speeds generally imply higher recording densities and faster transfer rates. The other is the average access time or the time it takes to get to any spot on the disk.

A recent innovation in diskette storage has doubled the amount of information stored on each (density). This is known as dual-density and is a function of the diskette drive, not the diskette itself. It is done by squeezing the information more closely together on the diskette — more bytes per sector, more sectors per track, and more tracks per diskette. It increases the capacity of mini- and standard-floppies to 180 and 512 kilobytes, respectively. Yet another innovation allows information to be read to and written on both sides of the floppy, thereby doubling again the amount of information stored. This means that up to one megabyte (mega = million) of data can be stored on one dual-sided, dual-density floppy. This may sound like a lot, but don't be surprised if your on-line storage requirements run into the multi-megabyte range.

As the amount of information stored on a floppy increases, so do the backup and recovery problems in the event of diskette failure. Don't save money on diskettes. Buy the most expensive, highest quality diskettes you can find and they'll pay for themselves many times over in reliability.

Information is recorded on both serial and random access devices in the same way as music is on tape. The media are coated with a magnetic oxide material. To write information, the read/write head in the disk or tape drive passing over a given spot on the tape or disk sends out a pulse of energy that magnetizes a bit of the material. Conversely, to read the information, the magnetized bits of material passing over the read/write head set up signals in the head that are passed to the computer. These discrete signals are combined in the computer to form numbers and characters in a way described more fully in the next chapter. However, the pattern of magnetic spots on either tape or disk can be easily disrupted by heat, moisture, cold, dryness, static, or magnetic fields. (I erase my diskettes with one of those little fruit magnets used to tack up messages on the refrigerator door.) Therefore, great care should be exercised in the storage of your disk and tape media.

The next step up from floppies is the hard disk. This is a rigid platter mounted in a drive. The removable ones are generally protected by a rigid package to prevent damage. They have higher recording densities than floppies and are even more sensitive to damage. The most common form of hard disk drive holds 10 megabytes of data on two platters, one of which is fixed in the drive and one of which is removable. This feature allows you to store all of your programs and operating software on one platter and all your data on another. This makes it easy to store data "off-line." The data transfer rates are also 5 to 10 times faster than those of floppies. (They are also 5 to 10 times more expensive than floppies.) Capacities range from 2½ to 15 megabytes per drive. Many systems will support multiple drives, but the access and recording principles are exactly the same as in floppies.

Finally, there are the Winchester-type drives. This is the latest revolution in storage devices. They are just like regular rigid disks except that they are not removable. They are sealed into their drives in a dust-free environment and are (or should be) quality engineered to run almost indefinitely without failure. The biggest problem with Winchester-type drives, which led to a serious marketing failure when they first appeared, is backup. All data on a computer system must be regularly and frequently copied onto some other storage device so that in the event of a failure of the storage medium the lost data can be recovered. In the case of floppy disks and removable hard disks, this is easy. Just buy an extra disk for every operational disk and make copies by inserting the backup into a second drive and copying the files over. When you are unable to remove the disk, however, what do you do? Since the Winchesters — which come in 5¼-, 8-, and 14-inch diameters — can store from 6 to 30 megabytes, copying this information to floppy disks would take too much time, money, and diskette space. Recovering lost data would take just as much time. Solving this problem has led to the development and popularization of the cartridge tape drive. With high speed transfer rates and large capacities (3 to 37 megabytes), cartridge tape drives are the ideal solution to the backup problem.

INTERFACE BOARDS

The problem with all peripheral devices (input, output, and storage) is that the electrical signals coming from them to the computer are not recognizable by the computer, and signals from the computer look like gibberish to the peripheral. To overcome this problem, a circuit board must be placed between it and the processor. The function of this board is to translate the signals going either way so that they will be comprehensible to the receiving component: processor or peripheral. These translator boards are known as "interfaces." They make it possible to hook peripheral devices from different manufacturers to different computers. If you are using the turnkey approach to the purchase of a system, you don't need to worry about interface boards; your system will come with all you need. However, if you are using the adventurous method, read on.

The interface boards are usually located inside the computer. Generally, one board is required for each device. Be sure that the processor's chassis has enough slots in it to accommodate as many boards as you'll need to service the peripheral devices you require initially or may want in the future. Some processors offer an optional expansion chassis for more memory or interface boards, which means you can start small and expand later without having to anticipate every possibility.

Finally, don't forget the cost of the interface when pricing your system or considering a new peripheral. The price of the peripheral usually does not include the price of the interface and this can be substantial.

Figure 13. A typical microcomputer system, Pertec's PCC2000. The two diskette drives are located to the right of the CRT screen. A impact printer is shown to the left. (Courtesy of PERTEC Computer Corp.)

34

Figure 14. Vendor ranking — Installed computer systems among small businesses (Courtesy Time, Inc.)

35

VENDORS AND COSTS

Because of the rapid advances in technology and the equally rapid expansion of the small business computer industry, both vendors and hardware prices are difficult to write about. Prices tend to change radically in short periods of time — both up, due to inflation, and down, due to economies of scale, new and cheaper manufacturing processes, and competitive pressures. At the low end of the spectrum are systems like Radio Shack and Apple Computers. For $3–$4 thousand you can get a complete system with floppy disks and printer suitable for basic business applications. The high end can take you well over $50 thousand for systems with hard disks and multiple terminals. The majority of the tabletop microcomputer–based small business systems with floppy disk drives will fall in the $10–$20 thousand price range. Use Appendix A as a guide to pricing your hardware.

VENDOR	# SYSTEMS (000)	SHARE	CUMULATIVE
IBM	38.8	33.8%	33.8%
Burroughs	11.7	10.2	44.0
NCR	8.0	7.0	51.0
DEC	6.8	5.9	56.9
Basic Four	5.6	4.9	61.8
Philips	4.6	4.0	65.8
Data General	4.5	3.9	69.7
Wang	2.2	1.9	71.6
Univac	2.0	1.7	73.3
Honeywell	2.0	1.7	75.0
Data Point	2.0	1.7	76.7
Olivetti	1.8	1.6	78.0
Hewlett-Packard	1.7	1.5	79.8
Qantel	1.6	1.4	81.2
Texas Instruments	1.1	1.0	82.2
Cado	1.1	1.0	83.2
Microdata	1.0	.9	84.1
Four Phase	.9	.8	84.9
All Others	17.5	15.1	100.0
Total	114.9	100.0%	

Projected Universe: 1,711,357 small businesses in industries with the highest potential for computer utilization.

Figure 15. Vendor ranking — Installed computer systems among small businesses. (Source: "Small Computers for Small Business," Time, Inc./Focus Research study 1980; reprinted with permission.)

As for vendors, Figure 15 shows the current ranking of the most popular vendors. I would expect significant changes in this list over the next few years. Neither Tandy (Radio Shack), Apple, nor Xerox appears on the list. Some vendors will become victims of a shake-out as competitive pressures reduce margins and drive the less efficient manufacturers out of the field. There is nothing wrong with buying hardware from a vendor not on the list. Just be sure that (1) they have been around long enough for you to be confident that they won't be going out of business (you'll need the service support) and (2) their hardware has been in the field long enough to have had the bugs worked out of it (you don't want to be a guinea pig or a test site for someone's untried hardware).

A FINAL WORD

The purpose of gaining familiarity with the various types of hardware is that you won't be so distracted by them when you go shopping for a computer system. Understandably, you will at first be able to relate much more easily to these toys than to the unseeable and intangible programs that run inside them. And you will have a natural tendency to overshop for the hardware and neglect the software selection process. Please try to think of the hardware as an accessory to the system you are buying. Or think of it this way: Software is to hardware as a TV program is to a TV. You don't really watch your TV, do you?

Unit	Usage	Capacity Range	Data Handling Speed	Price Range
Disk				
Mini-floppy diskette (5¼ inches)	Small files	50,000–120,000 characters	400 millisecond access	$350–$900
Full-size floppy diskette (8 inches)	Small/medium files	120,000–600,000 characters	100–400 millisecond access	$700–$1,800
Winchester (8-inch disk)	Medium files	6–10 million characters	80–200 millisecond access	$2,500–$6,000
Winchester (14-inch disk)	Medium/large files	15–30 million characters	50–120 millisecond access	$3,000–$7,000
Cartridge disk removable	Medium files	2.5–15 million characters	70–150 millisecond access	$3,500–$8,000
Module disk drive	Large files	50–180 million characters	35–90 millisecond access	$8,000–$15,000
Pack disk drive	Super files	200–600 million characters	25–70 millisecond access	$15,000–$45,000
Magnetic Tape				
Reel-to-reel	Logging, archives, and backup computer–computer transfer	20–120 million characters	12.5–125 inches per second	$2,000–$20,000
Cartridge tape	Logging, archives and backup	3–37 million characters	15–90 inches per second	$800–$3,000
Cassette tape	Logging and small archives	50–150,000 characters	1–7/8 inches per second	$300–$1,000

Printers				
Serial/character	Slow reports and transaction documents	50–260 characters per line	30–300 characters per second	$600–$8,000
Letter quality	Documents and letters	80–132 characters per line	15–55 characters per second	$2,000–$4,500
Line	Bulk reports	120–132 characters per line	200–6,000 lines per minute	$6,000–$15,000
High speed	Major report production	132 characters per line	1,100–2,400 lines per minute	$10,000–$35,000
Terminals				
CRT	Data input and query	600–8,000 characters per screen	30–1,920 characters per second	$600–$2,000
Keyboard printer	Input/transaction documents	50–132 characters per line	30–1,920 characters per second	$1,200–$3,000
Color CRT	Data input and query	2,000–4,000 characters per screen	30–1,920 characters per second	$2,000–$6,000
Graphics	Drawings and data inputs	10,000–30,000 graphic points per screen	30–1,920 characters per second	$3,000–$10,000

Table 1. Small Computer Peripheral Alternatives. (Reprinted from the May, 1980 issue of *Small Systems World*, by permission of Hunter Publishing Company)

3

SYSTEM SOFTWARE

INTRODUCTION

The distinction between hardware and software is fairly simple but fundamental. Hardware includes all the equipment we discussed in the last chapter — disks, printers, processors; anything you can lay your hands on. Software is programs. Where is a program? Physically the program is stored in the computer's memory in the form of a series of instructions. Since the memory is so tiny, the physical existence of the program in terms of microscopic charges of electricity takes up a correspondingly small place in the world. Since most of the rest of the book concerns software, there certainly must be much more to it than this.

Where is a television program? Certainly it is more than the charges on the surface of the TV screen or the videotape. Close your eyes and picture a rose. Where is that rose? (Certainly not painted on the inside of your forehead.) Go ahead; do it.

Like the rose, the program in a computer has no tangible existence. Yet, like the rose, we can see it — if we print it out on the printer (we can paint a picture of the rose we pictured). The real existence of programs — software — is in the abstraction. We know what we want done. We tell the computer in terms it can understand. It saves our instructions and repeats them over and over again at our command, exactly the same way each time. So how, then, does the computer store anything?

BITS, BYTES, AND BINARY CONVERSATIONS

The fundamental building block of the computer is a semiconductor, a device that acts as a switch. This implies, correctly, that this switch can take on one of two states. Never mind about the physics of the device and how it works. Suffice it to say that these semiconductor devices can take on one of two states, which we can call "on" and "off," "high" and "low," "zero" and "one," and so on. Note that in changing from one state to another, the switch does not move. In other words, these are solid state devices. But the nature of the electrical state inside the device does change.

The computer is full of solid state devices — the devices are differentiated to do different tasks, but all essentially operate in the same fashion: "on" or "off" and "zero" or "one." If you are a programmer, you have control over all the switches. You can make them take on any value you like and make decisions based on the values. Oh, yes, these switches can alternate between the two states at unbelievable speeds.

Since there are two physical states that a semiconductor can assume, it is natural that numbers in a computer be expressed in binary, or base two. In fact, at its most elementary level, the internal representation of data, programs, or what have you, is binary in all computers. Now, if we take a group of these switches and string them together, they can be used to represent a number in binary. For example, four switches that read one, zero, zero, one would represent the number 1001 in binary, which equals 9 in decimal, our familiar base 10 numbering system. Given enough switches, any number can be represented.

The zeros and ones, the most elementary units in the computers, are referred to as binary digits, or "bits" for short. Eight of these bits together is called a "byte," which is the unit of information most often referred to. I have 32,768 bytes of memory in my computer. My diskette can hold 90,000 bytes.

There are 256 combinations of zero and one that can be formed from a string of 8 bits. So any number from 0 (00000000) to 255 (11111111) can be represented in a byte.

In all computers, 26 of these combinations have been arbitrarily assigned to represent the letters of the alphabet; 10 more have been assigned to the numbers 0 to 9. From computer to computer, the combinations so selected may vary. But in most cases they will be the same, conforming to a standard known as "ASCII," the American Standard Code for Information Interchange. Several other combinations have been reserved for special characters. In this fashion, words, text, numbers, or other alphanumeric information can be stored in the computer as strings of ones and zeros.

The printer, which you will hook to your computer through an interface, is wired so that when these numbers stream out of the computer, the printer (which knows what the code stands for) prints the right character. Numbers also must have a special set of codes so they can be printed. The CRT (the screen on which information is displayed) is set up in the same way, so that when the codes come to the CRT from the computer, they are translated by the CRT's character-generating circuits into letters, numbers, and special characters that you can read.

If you find all this a bit confusing, just think of a byte as a character. If there are 2,648 characters (including spaces and punctuation) on this page, then it would take 2,468 bytes to store this page in a computer.

Special combinations of these bits and bytes serve a second purpose in the computer. They represent the instructions or commands the computer uses to perform its work. For example, one 8-bit combination might signal the computer to add 2 numbers together. Another 8-bit combination would make the computer compare 2 numbers setting another bit switch to "on" or "off" − depending on whether the first number was larger or smaller than the second number. A third 8-bit combination might tell the computer to jump to a different part of the program if the bit set in the last instruction is a one and not a zero.

The number of different combinations that a given computer recognizes is its instruction set and to a great degree determines the power of the computer. For example, one computer may have one instruction telling the computer to add 2 numbers in its memory together and store them in a third place in the memory. A much less powerful computer without this instruction would have to: (1) load the first number into a temporary holding area known as a register, (2) load the second number into a second register, (3) add the contents of the two registers together, and (4) store the number back into the memory. The first computer did the same operations but only one instruction was needed to tell it what to do.

Now we're really getting somewhere. We can store data in the computer's memory, and instructions as well. These instructions, when executed by the computer in a logical sequence, will do something useful for us with the data.

Of course, you won't actually have to store the instructions yourself. A programmer will do it for you − a job for which they get paid very handsomely.

SPEAKING THE LANGUAGE

There are two problems with this binary language. First, it is the only language the computer really knows or understands, if you will, under which it can operate. Second, binary, which is also known as "machine language," is so difficult to program into a computer that it makes any kind of programming well nigh impossible. Nevertheless, this is how most of the first programs were written − in binary, with great pain.

Finally, someone invented a program called an assembler. It allows you to use alphabetic symbols instead of binary numbers to represent instructions and lets you refer to different pieces of data by key words of your own choosing. The assembler then takes your symbolic program and translates it for you into machine language. Very convenient, no? Now our ability to write longer, more complex programs is greatly enhanced. So popular was this approach that even today almost all computer manufacturers supply an assembler program with their machines (for a fee, of course).

I don't mean to sound ungrateful, but even with all its conveniences, programming in assembly language can be a big pain in the neck. You see, each line of code is translated into one, and only one, machine language instruction. Suppose I want to calculate the solution to the quadratic equation "$Z = AX^2 + BX + C$." This will take a great number of assembly language instructions to accomplish.

HIGHER LEVEL LANGUAGES

To overcome this problem, very elaborate programs have been written (most likely in assembler language) that allow you to use statements and commands that begin to look a little like English (!). This type of program, known as a compiler, takes your commands and translates them into hundreds or even thousands of machine language instructions. All the compiler asks of you is that you rigidly adhere to the strict rules of syntax that the program expects.

Now we really are getting somewhere. I can take the quadratic equation above and write "$Z = A*X**2 + B**$," which is how it would look according to the rules of syntax of one of the popular high-level languages. The compiler will create the machine language to do it. I can say "Input X, Y, Z," and the compiler will create the instructions to allow someone to input three values from the CRT. I can write "If X > Y Print X, Y," and the compiler will generate instructions to print X and Y only if the value of X is greater than the value of Y.

There are three popular higher level languages for small systems. Two, FORTRAN and COBOL, are compiler programs. The first is FORTRAN, or FORmula TRANslator. Its code is very compact and highly symbolic. It was initially designed for mathematical applications but is now gaining wider application in business. The second is COBOL, the COmmon Business-Oriented Language — one of the oldest computer languages. COBOL's forte is that it is self-documenting; that is, it reads almost like English, and when properly programmed, leaves little doubt as to what is being done. In FORTRAN, the names you use to represent certain pieces of information are limited to 6 characters, so that you might abbreviate a name which represents net profit margin as "NPMGN." Not very obvious, is it? In COBOL, the same variable could be written "Net–Profit–Margin." Of course, every time you refer to this variable in the COBOL program it must be written out, taking a lot of time and giving you the opportunity to make many errors.

Both of these languages are translated by compilers into machine language before they are run. The original form of the program in FORTRAN or COBOL is known as the "source program," and the compiled version (that is, the program in machine language) is the "object program" or object code.

A third language, and perhaps the most popular among users of microcomputers, is BASIC. BASIC operates a little differently than FORTRAN and COBOL. It is interpretive. This means that instead of your source program being compiled into machine language code, each source statement in your program (that is, everything you write in BASIC) is read by another program called the interpreter, and the machine language instructions to perform that statement are executed by the interpreter on the spot. The biggest advantage of BASIC is its ease of programming and debugging. Its primary disadvantage is that each manufacturer supplies a slightly different version of BASIC with its machine. BASIC also runs much slower than compiled programs. But in the case of small business systems, where the amount of information to be processed is not great, this is rarely a big problem.

Now that you understand something about how information and programs are stored in the computer, I would like to present a special class of programs: the system software. System programs are differentiated from the applications programs, which will be addressed in the next chapter. Applications programs perform some useful task that you have defined, such as printing payroll checks or keeping track of your inventory. The system software is programming that aids the applications program in doing its job. System software is generally supplied by the manufacturer of the computer. Applications software is provided by people who write programs for a living. This distinction will become clearer as we look at the major system programs.

THE OPERATING SYSTEM

The operating system is the traffic cop of the computer. It is a collection of programs that interfaces between the computer and the applications programs. Its responsibilities include starting and stopping jobs, accepting commands from the operator and executing them, i.e., controlling the input and output operations, and performing other common tasks.

When you turn your computer on, the first thing that generally happens is that the operating system is loaded into memory from the disk. Then control is handed over to the operating system, which displays some kind of descriptive message like "READY." At this point you are ready either to run an applications program or to perform one of the many handy tasks the operating system is capable of, If you say, for example, "RUN

PAYROLL," the operating system will go out to the disk, find the payroll program, load it into memory, and begin executing it. The payroll program and its data will use different parts of memory than that being used by the operating system. The system is said to be "resident." This means that it is there all the time, in case something in the payroll program requires its intervention. When the payroll program is finished, it returns control to the operating system, which then asks you for the next task.

Some of the more common functions of your operating system are:

1. Create a file.
2. Delete a file.
3. Save a program on disk.
4. Display a directory of all the programs on a disk.
5. Copy the contents of one file to another file.
6. Set the date and time in the computer's clock and send this information to any program requesting it.
7. Dump certain contents of memory to disk, printer, or CRT.
8. Show the amount of free space remaining on a disk.
9. Load a program into memory and start running it.
10. List a file's contents on the CRT or printer.
11. Rename a program or data file.
12. Display some sort of informative message to the user when an error occurs in the hardware or software.

As you can see, most of the functions are not only very convenient, eliminating the need to write programs to accomplish them, but they are also quite necessary to the functioning of your entire system.

When you are evaluating a computer for purchase, it will pay to thoroughly explore the functions and capabilities of the operating system. Even if you are buying a turnkey system, you will eventually want to perform some of the utility functions. Sophistication of a computer's operating system is one of the best measures of the overall capability of the computer.

UTILITIES

Utility programs are a subset of the system software that provide necessary services to the user. Many are mere extensions of the operating system functions just listed. The most common class of utilities performs the transfer of program and/or data files from one medium to another: transfer from tape to disk, transfer from disk to tape, copy from one file to another, list the contents from a file to the printer or CRT, or copy a whole disk. This last function, also known as a backup program, is one of the most important utilities because it forms the cornerstone of your system's security, making it easy and convenient for you to make copies of your data files for storage in case of a disk failure or catastrophic error (like zeroing out the year-to-date information in your general ledger a month too early).

After backup, sorting is probably the most useful utility in your system. In its ideal form it can be used two ways. First, it can be used as a stand-alone program; that is, it should prompt you for the file to be sorted and for the items within the file's records that should be used for sorting. Second, it can be called from within a program. The sort utility should allow you to specify several key fields on which to sort and whether those fields should sort in ascending or descending order.

If the system you are considering does not offer comprehensive sort capability, be sure to find out what the problems are in getting one. Does the computer manufacturer have one available or can they arrange for one? Can the supplier of the applications software provide one? Is a canned (already written, available off-the-shelf) package that is compatible with this machine and its file structure available from some third party?

TIMESHARING OR MULTIPROGRAMMING OR MULTITASKING OR MULTITERMINAL OPERATION OR CONCURRENT EXECUTION OR . . .

All these terms refer to the ability of an operating system to handle the simultaneous operation of more than one program and/or more than one terminal at a time. This implies that the operating system will be responsible for: (1) assigning a fixed amount of memory to a program and its data, thereby protecting it from use by other programs and preventing it from writing in someone else's area, and (2) resolving conflicts between users competing for the same resource, like a disk, by queueing them up and servicing them according to some predetermined rules of priority.

One of the primary differences between the very small low-cost business systems ($5–$20 thousand) and the medium range systems ($15–$500 thousand) is the ability not only of the hardware to accept several terminals at one time, but also of the system software to accommodate them. If you plan to implement so many different functions on your computer that it appears they cannot all be done in one day by one person performing them sequentially, then you will want to evaluate systems that allow several users simultaneous access to the computer and its resources. (Recently, multi-terminal operating systems have appeared for small systems. As time goes by, those with more of the capabilities of medium-sized systems will appear in small systems.)

When several users are on a multiterminal system, each of the users gets quick response from the computer, giving them the impression that they have the machine all to themselves. What makes this possible is the enormous difference in speed between the internal operations of the computer and the speed of input and output operations (transfers of data to and from the disk, inputs by the user through the keyboard, displays on the CRT, and/or printing), even though in actuality only one user can be executing instructions at any one time.

When a user asks for a record from disk, the operating system takes over and sends a request to the disk for the record. The time it takes for the disk to respond, even though it is only a few hundred milliseconds, seems like a whole afternoon to the computer. While waiting, the computer has enough time to service all of the other users on the system up to the point in their programs where they are waiting on a slow input or output operation.

Of course, as the number of users on a system grows, the amount of time the operating system spends keeping track of their resource requests grows and the less time it has to spend actually doing the user's work. This is known as "thrashing," and if the operating system is not efficient, this can eat up a considerable amount of time, thus slowing the response time to all the users. If you intend to buy a machine that supports several terminals for simultaneous operation, be sure to run a test of the software by getting together enough people to run the maximum number of terminals you intend to have. In this way you'll be able to judge how well the computer will respond under heavy load conditions.

DISTRIBUTED DATA PROCESSING

Distributed Data Processing (DDP) is the latest in buzz words. It means many different things to many people. Like all real new terms in the computer industry its eventual definition has not yet been arrived at. However, since you will doubtless hear this term repeatedly in your search for the perfect system, I will try to shed a little light on the subject.

The most common data processing arrangement for big companies using big computers used to be the central computer site. Close at hand was a room full of keypunches — machines which punch holes in the familiar "punched card." All day, source documents like inventory transfers, payroll time cards, sales orders, and the like would come pouring into the keypunch room to be punched onto cards and fed into the computers. The printed reports would then be delivered from the computer room printers to the users.

The development of terminals meant that the users, using terminals in their own departments, connected to the central computer by long cables, could input their transactions directly into the computer. A lot of keypunchers were put out of work. (However, they were needed to do the terminal input work in the users' departments. Thus, a new job was born — the data entry clerk.) The input function was "distributed" away from the central site to the remotely located users.

Placing remote printers in the user's own area and programming the computer to send the output there *distributed* the output function. The responsibilities for the input and output were also distributed to the users. This arrangement preserved the biggest advantage of the central site — everyone had access to all the data. As the number of users and terminals increased, so did the load on the central processor, increasing the time it took for each user to get a response from the central computer.

The development of small, cheap processors and diskette technology gave systems designers a way out — distribute the processing load by giving each department their own computer; one in payroll, one in purchasing, one in receivables, one in inventory, etc. The problem here, of course, is that it is very difficult to consolidate your information if it's spread all over the company. If the accounts payable clerk needs to see a purchase order, a trip to the purchasing department is necessary.

Figure 16 shows the arrangement that solves this problem: Distributed processors, each one actually a complete microcomputer system with CRT, keyboard, microprocessor, diskettes, and printer, are all hooked to a hard disk. If you need more than one terminal in your business, this is the arrangement you will probably end up with. Its advantages include modular expansion (you can add more microcomputers as you need them), centralized data storage (everyone gets to see all the data), and distribution of the processing load. The disk controller, which has its own microprocessor, "knows" where information is coming from and where to send it when requests for data come to it from one of the microcomputers.

Since each system can have its own diskettes for local storage, this arrangement represents true Distributed Data Processing — distribution of the input, the output, the processing, and the storage.

ACCESS METHODS

The power of a computer resides in its ability to retrieve information in a fast, orderly manner. To do this, it must be able to store it in a *fast* and *orderly* manner. Just as the input/output devices discussed in the hardware section can be broken into two broad categories, *sequential* and *random,* so can the access methods of the software system be broken down the same way. Serial access can be used on random access storage devices — disks and diskettes. Random access is ill-suited to serial devices like tapes however, since a request for any record in the file would require a sequential scan from the beginning of the file. In either case, it is another piece of system software that handles the operation.

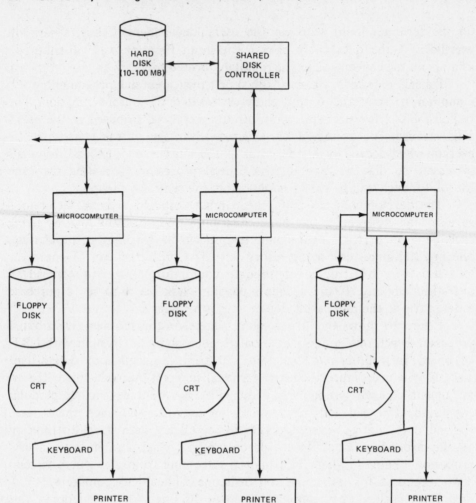

Figure 16. System diagram of a Distributed Data Processing system.

In the early days of programming, this was not so. If you wanted to store names and addresses on a disk and be able to retrieve them in name sequence, you had to write a subroutine for your program to do this. Your main program would then pass a name to the subroutine, whose job it would be to calculate where on the disk this particular record resided and go out and get it. This type of keyed access is quite difficult to write. Now, most machines have system software to provide this capability.

This program requests that a particular record be stored on disk and specifies to the I/O (Input/Output) control program which part of the record it should use as a key. The I/O control program then takes over, storing the record in such a way that when you later request that this record be retrieved, all you have to do is use the key and it retrieves the record for you. For example, you want to see the inventory information for part number "P8346." Your program will pass the key value "P8346" to the I/O control program, which will go to the disk, find the record that has the key value "P8346," and send it back to the computer's memory where the program can then display it for you on the CRT.

This access method is most often referred to as ISAM (Indexed Sequential Access Method) or KSAM (Keyed Sequential Access Method). Both terms refer to programs that can store and retrieve records based on a key value. The word "sequential" refers to the fact that this program can also retrieve the next record in the key sequence without having to specify the key. For example, if you ask for the record of "Brown, Mary," it will fetch it for you. You can then say to the ISAM, "Get the next record in sequence," and it will fetch "Browser, Fred," and so on. In this way, a file that is indexed (or keyed) by name can be retrieved in alphabetical order, even though it was created in a random order.

The capabilities of the access method of your software system will set limits on the efficiency of the programs you put on it (in terms of time for storage and retrieval of data and the amount of space required for that data on the disk). Since most business applications are heavily weighted in favor of input and output (as opposed to calculating), this feature of the system software becomes quite important.

Next to ISAM, sequential access is simple. In sequential output, the next record written is tacked onto the end of the file. In sequential input, the next record is read in sequence. Although this seems, compared to ISAM, to be an I/O method that has very limited capability, there are times when having the ability to store and retrieve by keys is unnecessary. The simplicity of sequential access also means less work for the operating system and, hence, faster response. Under random access, the ISAM must first calculate the location of the record and then move the read/write heads of the disk to that track. In sequential retrieval, the read/write head is almost always correctly positioned already. Finally, sequential files take up less room on a disk. Both methods have their place in the applications programs you will be buying. Which one is used will depend on the designers and programmers of these applications.

System software is probably the most difficult topic to understand. Yet its importance can be likened to your metabolism. Whatever you do for a living is your "application program," but unless your operating system, your heart, lungs, brain, etc., are operating smoothly and efficiently, you won't get any work done at all.

Figure 17. The desk top IBM 5120 computer system has the power of a computer that 20 years ago would have filled a 20 by 30 foot room and weighed a ton. Slots to the right of the screen hold 8-inch floppy disks. (Courtesy of IBM)

4

APPLICATIONS SOFTWARE – SOME GENERAL PRINCIPLES

INTRODUCTION

This chapter will explain some of the general features of applications software: what to look for in applications software; how to judge the quality of the software you're looking at; and how to avoid some of the common pitfalls of buying, installing, and using these programs.

The quality of the computer hardware you will be looking at has advanced so rapidly over the last few years that it has far outstripped the quality of the software that is available for these machines. The same thing is happening to the hardware side of the stereo business. Unless you take a lot of time to study the specs, are an engineer, or like to hang out in listening rooms full of speakers in stereo stores, I'll bet you could more easily tell the difference between a Bud and a Michelob than a Pioneer and a Kenwood. What has happened is that the technology of sound reproduction for the home is far better than the signal that most of the records, tapes, and radio stations provide.

Likewise with computer hardware. If you stick with the reputable brands, they're essentially the same. In fact, the less of your time and attention the hardware requires, the happier you are.

Just as we see television in terms of the programs that appear on the screen and not the circuitry behind it, so, as users of small business systems, do we regard computers in terms of the programs that are in them and how they perform. This means that proportionately more effort should go into the selection of software than hardware and proportionately more work should go into understanding the programs and how they operate.

In a very real sense, then, what you buy when you computerize are the programs. The hardware is simply an accessory that you must buy to help your software run.

HOW TO BUY IT

Rarely before has the phrase "caveat emptor" (buyer beware) had such significance. The ratio of good to bad business software has been close to zero since the advent of small business systems. Only very recently has the line lifted its shabby head off the "X" axis. What this means to you, the buyer, is that your chances of getting a decent piece of software on the recommendation of a computer store sales person are exactly two: slim and none. As for ordering business software by mail on the strength of the advertising, I would sooner do something less risky, like playing the commodities market. Yet it never ceases to amaze me how many otherwise conservative people who wouldn't buy a T-shirt without a fitting will plunk down their business' scarce capital for a diskette of programs on the strength of the advertiser's claims and/or the reviews they read in the hobby magazines. They then proceed to disrupt their entire business trying to figure out from the incomprehensible documentation just how the stuff is supposed to work, and then spend even more time trying to make their business operate around a set of business procedures that they would never think of putting into a manual system.

In my opinion, there is only one way to buy software and that is to try it before you buy it. It is laborious and time-consuming — a pain in the neck, if we're to be honest about it. But it will provide you with not only the program you need to do your job, but also with a first-rate education in business systems that will stand you in good stead later in your implementation. Here are the steps you should follow when you buy your software:

1.   Once you have identified a likely candidate for evaluation — either from a trade show, magazine article, review, or personal recommendation — find two or three people who have been using this program long enough to know its strong and weak points. Call them up, or better yet, see them where the program is being used and watch it operate. If it is difficult to find these people, the store that sells the program should be able to recommend a few satisfied clients. The company that manufacturers it should also be able to help you. If you can find no one who is able or willing to set you up with a few seasoned users of this particular package, and you're not imbued with the true trailblazing spirit of a hobbyist, do not buy this program.

It isn't necessary for their business to be the same as yours, but the business needs should be similar. If you are a parts distributor, try to find another distributor with similar inventory problems. If you're a service professional (doctor, dentist, accountant, or architect), try to find another professional whose accounting requirements parallel yours. Ask them how they like it, what problems they have had, whether the documentation is adequate, and what they would like it to do or thought it would do that it doesn't (there's always something). The system you're looking at should have been operating in this business for at least one accounting cycle.

Discount these reports by the ego factor (which makes people want to look as if they made the right decision). If the program passes this test to your satisfaction, go on to step 2.

2. Next, locate some hardware as close as possible in configuration to what you're eventually going to call your own. It is preferable to choose one on which this particular software has already been implemented and one that you can use on evenings, weekends, or off hours without feeling pressed for time. (I am assuming that you have not committed the cardinal sin of buying your hardware before embarking on a software search. Remember that the software you eventually settle on will to a great extent limit your hardware choices — perhaps even to a single vendor.)

The best place to make these arrangements is at the computer store or dealership that is selling the hardware/software combination you're interested in. If you can't make these arrangements with either the dealer or a relatively close user, I would be very skeptical of this particular package.

Borrow the manuals describing the operation of the programs you are considering and read them. Don't expect to be able to learn all about the system from the manuals. This is almost impossible even for the best written manuals. Generally they are designed to be used for reference more than training. Therefore, check the table of contents and index closely.

If they are such gobbledygook that it seems you'll need some serious handholding to make the programs work right, you might want to think twice about this package. Poor documentation is one of the surest signs of low quality software. Don't buy any undocumented software!! If the documentation has not been written yet, it means that the software is not a finished product. You will be used as a guinea pig to find the bugs in the programs.

3. Assemble enough test data from your own business to experience all the different features of the software. In the case of accounts receivable, for example, bring along regular invoices, sales orders, and debit and credit memos. Bring this data to the computer on the same documents that you are presently using. This way you'll know if your source documents have all the information required by the system, how hard it will be to enter the information from them, and whether you'll have to redesign your form or your manual system to fit the procedures of this particular program.

Input this raw data into the system, paying attention to how easily the prompts that appear on the screen lead you through the process, how fast the computer responds after you input a transaction, and whether all the information the program asks for is present on your existing source documents.

Good prompts will leave little doubt in your mind as to what the program is asking for. For example, when entering an invoice, the prompt "Amount?" is too vague. "Total invoice amount?," "Extended dollars?," "Unit price?," or "$ Amount of this line item?," would all be more precise, hence, superior.

The response time — that is, the time elapsed between the end of the item you input and the next prompt appearing on the screen — should be fast enough to keep you from getting anxious and to allow the input to proceed smoothly. All of the prompts for a given transaction — that is, all of the information required by the program for one invoice or to record one inventory change — should appear with almost no discernable pause. The time between transactions (between invoices or inventory changes) will be longer, but by no more than a few seconds at most. Some systems will take 10 to 60 seconds to process a transaction. I judge this to be unacceptable.

If the response time is too slow, it generally means the programs have been written in an inefficient way. The most likely source of slowness is the routine that transfers information to and from the disk. This lag cannot generally be made up by putting the same program on a faster computer. As I said earlier, within a given price range, all the hardware is about the same.

4.   Run through the entire cycle of programs. Simulate a whole month's activity if you can. Go through the end-of-month features of the program, if there are any, and the end-of-year routines. Generate all the reports. Is everything there that you need? Are the audit trails satisfactory; that is, if the computer goes dead for 2 weeks, has it left enough printed information of its activity behind to allow you to reconstruct your business manually? Have you found any soft bugs (meaning ones that do not stop the computer cold, but give an incorrect or misleading response or result)? If so, what does the company marketing the program say about providing you with a fix (for the problem, that is)? If they do fix it, retest it. Perform a backup procedure (see the next section for an explanation of this process). Does it meet your stringently paranoid suspicions about Murphy and his law?

5.   If the program still meets with your approval, go back and do the whole thing over again, this time deliberately trying to break the system. Hit the wrong keys. Give erroneous responses. Put in numbers for letters, and vice versa. Do everything wrong you can possibly think of. Be creative. Try to pay an accounts payable twice. Overpay an employee. Try to throw

the general ledger out of balance. Turn the system off in the middle of a critical process. Did it destroy your data files? How hard is it to recover from your errors? Are errors easily identifiable? How much help did you get from the program? I don't mean to suggest here that the only good program is one that can pass this test. No program is completely foolproof. You are just trying to discover the weaknesses of the program and whether or not you can live with them.

If you get all the way through this procedure and still like the program, it's probably the one for you. Try it on at least two other software systems if you can find them.

Any seller of commercial software worth doing business with will welcome your rigorous test of their programs. If the programs fail, good vendors will be able to upgrade their programs to do the job correctly. If they pass your test, you'll become a solid gold recommendation for their products.

BACKUP, AUDIT TRAILS, AND DISASTER RECOVERY

An audit trail (also referred to as a transaction listing) is a record of everything that has happened on your system. This can take the form of a printout on your printer or a file on your disk. It should show the date, time of day (if your machine has a clock), what the transaction was (cash receipt, check printed, customer added to the file, credit limit altered), and any inventory quantities and dollar amounts involved. It should also show altered records in both their old and new forms. The printed reports provide a hard-copy record of all the activity in your system and are your ultimate security in case of system failures.

Audit trails were originally implemented on large systems to provide protection against rip-offs, mostly from inside the company, and to provide a means for auditors to trace back all of the activity on the system to verify its correctness. Although security of data files should be as great a concern to you as security of your personal and business files, this is not the primary purpose of audit trails or transaction listings on a small business system. Their main function, quite frankly, is to enable you to recover when your system fails.

Note carefully, I said when and not if. I have worked on many different systems over the years and they all have one thing in common: they all fail (invariably at the worst time, destroying the most critical data files and wiping out important programs). I have never seen a system that was truly "foolproof." There is always some improper procedure to follow that was not and could not be anticipated by the creators of the system, and of course, data can always be entered incorrectly.

Although all prudent users of computers should be making regular backup copies of their data files in case of hardware, software, or procedural failures, it will happen sooner or later that your backup diskettes will fail, an irate customer will contest the amount of an invoice, unpaid invoices will be entered as paid, or someone will spill a soda in your disk drive. Any one of a thousand unlikely occurrences will happen. At that time, you will want to be able to go back and see exactly what was put into the system and the audit trails will be the only way to do this. Even in the event of a catastrophic failure of your hardware, the last complete status report, coupled with listings of all activity since the report, will enable you to reconstruct your files manually and hence maintain your billing, cash flow, inventory, payroll, etc.

There seems to be a prevailing philosophy among designers of very small business systems that this sort of feature is an unnecessary extravagance. It takes a lot of time to program and makes the programs bigger than they normally would be, decreasing the amount of memory available for data and increasing the difficulty of debugging. It's also tedious and boring to write and takes some knowledge of good accounting practices to successfully design and implement. The greatest objection, however, is that it is unjustified in view of the small amount of data typically saved in small systems. Don't believe it. Microprocessors are powerful enough (given the right software) to handle data bases containing millions of bytes of information. (Remember in the chapter on hardware how much data one could store in hard disks, Winchester-type drives, and even floppies and cartridges?) You can store hundreds of customers, thousands of inventory items, and years of historical information.

If the system you are considering does not have audit trails already, be prepared for a disaster by implementing a backup plan of your own before you computerize. Here are some of the things you might do to greatly increase the physical security of your data at very little expense or effort.

1.   Buy lots of diskettes with your system, more than you ever think you'll need. The first thing you should do when you turn on your system for the first time is to make copies of every program and file on every diskette that came with your system. This should be easily done with the vendor-supplied backup utility. Put these copies away in the company safe or locked in a file, somewhere out of the area where the computer is (to provide physical security in case of fire, flood, or riot). Better yet, take them home, well away from your place of business. In the event of the ultimate disaster, you can always rent or borrow a machine like yours and bring your data back to life.

2.   There will be an initial period during your implementation when you will be building your files up with all sorts of information that will

will be input only once (hopefully). These files include such things as the customer name and address file for your accounts receivable, the vendor name and address file for accounts payable, the employee information for payroll, and the initial description of the items in your inventory and their current quantities. A considerable effort will be expended getting these files created. When they are complete, you should make another copy of your data and store it off-site, away from your place of business.

3. Now, for every diskette you have with data on it, create two backup diskettes. At the end of each day, copy all data diskettes to their respective backup diskettes, alternating between the two backup diskettes so that on any given day you have your current files, yesterday's files, and the files from 2 days ago.

At the end of each week, bring the backups you keep at home to work, make a copy, and take them home again. At the end of your fiscal year, after you've closed the books, make another copy, put them together with the audit trails and transaction listings if your system creates them, and store them as you would your tax records.

4. Write the date of initial creation on each diskette. Over the course of the second year, discard the old diskettes on their birthdays and replace them with fresh diskettes.

In addition to the above procedures, you should have outlined, at least in your mind but preferably on paper, how it is that you're going to bring each data file up to date in the very real likelihood that you will have to go back to yesterday's file, or the day before yesterday's, or even to the weekly backup. In other words, if your accounts receivable file fails and the directory on yesterday's backup got messed up making the whole diskette unreadable, and your cat ruined the day before yesterday's backup, and you've brought last Friday's backup diskette from home and copied it over to your working diskette — how are you going to reconstruct all the activity that went on in your receivables system since last Friday night?

Of course, if your system creates audit trails or transaction listings, you're in good shape (provided, of course, that you had the foresight to set up an organized system for storing these reports in an orderly and disciplined way). If you've forgotten about the audit trails because you never thought that all those failures could occur at once, well, you might be in serious trouble.

Now this may sound like a very elaborate scheme, but let's look at what's really involved. Every day the backups take a couple of minutes each; once a week, an extra set of backups; once a year, another set. The expense is minimal: a couple of dozen diskettes at most. The time spent is not burdensome for the benefit it returns. What is difficult about this system is the discipline. The backup schedule must be rigidly adhered to no matter what the pressures of the day. I guarantee that you will use these backups, maybe as often as once a week. Sometimes you will lose a data file by accidentally deleting it or you will lose part of a file, deleting many records unintentionally or by error. Sometimes you will just want to go back to yesterday's files to verify something. Sometimes someone will input a great deal of data incorrectly, making it easier to go back one day and do it over than to try to correct the erroneous data. And, of course, you must expect both diskettes and tape to fail physically from time to time.

When this happens, part of the diskette or disk or tape becomes unreadable. If this unreadable spot on the recording surface is in a little-used file, it may escape detection for a while. But remember, each time you do a backup, you read the entire diskette, and you are verifying that all the data files are present in readable form.

Finally, do not be mislead into thinking that the existence of comprehensive audit trails obviates the necessity of a rigorous backup procedure. Copying yesterday's backup diskette to the failed diskette takes a few minutes. No more than one day's input will be required to recover from the failure. If you only do monthly backups, then a diskette failure toward the end of the month will require re-inputting the entire month's activity. Audit trails are your *ultimate* security, not your first line of defense.

What do you get in return from your minimal but disciplined effort and $100 to $200 worth of diskettes per year? It is far cheaper than any business insurance you could buy that would provide your business enough compensation to make up for the lost data. Remember, if your automation is successful, you are now depending heavily on the continued presence of those files and the machine that makes them accessible. So you also get peace of mind; the kind of peace of mind you get when you know that your business is being run in a disciplined, well-controlled manner.

What should you expect from a commercial business system in the way of backup and recovery provisions? As you can tell from the above discussion, I regard system backup procedures critical to a successful operation. However, since this procedural topic falls mainly outside of the area of hardware and software, most vendors leave this pretty much to the discretion of the individual user. A top-notch business system will have both a section in the documentation on backup and security procedures, and prompts on the screen telling the operator how and when to do the backups. It shows a concern for the user by the writers of the system and a pragmatic realization that their market is comprised mainly of unsophisticated users who require this kind of advice and training in order to successfully integrate a computer into their businesses.

BATCH VERSUS ON-LINE PROCESSING

The distinction between batch processing and on-line processing represents a significant philosophical difference in the way a system is designed and in the way it operates for you. There is certainly a place for both in the world of small business systems. It is important for you to know what approach has been taken by the creators of the software you are considering buying. Each has advantages and disadvantages, which may be more or less important to you depending on the way you run your business, what your need for information is, and even your personality.

In batch processing, a whole group of transactions is input to the computer and, after being checked by the program for accuracy and reasonableness, is stored in a temporary or holding file. When the last transaction has been input, the program generally prompts for some kind of total figure for the whole batch of transactions, perhaps total hours worked for all employees' time cards entered into the payroll system or the total dollars of sales. This batch figure will have been precalculated by a human. If this figure does not match the running total kept by the program, you will have to go back and correct one or more transactions (or perhaps correct the batch total calculated by the human). Hopefully, the program will be designed to allow you to go back and "edit" your work.

You can see the big advantage here. Where accuracy is critical as in accounts payable, for example, you allow the computer to check the accuracy of your work and advise corrective action when necessary.

The next step in batch processing may also be a big advantage for you. After the temporary transaction file is ready, another program, the update program, takes over and processes these transactions. This may mean updating the employee's payroll quarter-to-date and year-to-date fields and preparing a check, or it may create invoices. It may update the quantity-on-hand fields for a whole batch of inventory receipts or it may overlay the totals from all the subsidiary ledgers, payroll, receivables, payables, etc., to your general ledger. While it is doing all this work, you can leave the machine unattended.

Batch systems can cause problems in the increased complexity of the procedures that must be followed exactly in order to make the system work properly. I have seen many batches of transactions lost because the operator of the system forgot to run the update program. There are systems so designed that they will allow the updating to be done twice on the same data, resulting in double postings of payroll, or payables, or receivables. When following the checkout procedure outlined above in the section on how to buy software, deliberately try to subvert the batch processing procedures. You will discover for yourself whether this feature of batch processing will cause you problems.

Another problem with batch systems occurs when the hardware fails. Since it often happens in the middle of processing a batch of transactions, there is no way to know which transactions have been completed and which remain to be done. Generally, this means you will have to go back to a backup diskette, copy over the transaction file, or, if it is unavailable, re-enter all the transactions and run the programs again.

However, the biggest disadvantage with batch processing is that when you look at your files at any point in time you are not seeing the true, up-to-date picture. Now, in some cases this is a trivial problem. When you are checking an employee's payroll status, how their records looked last Friday night is probably timely enough information. But if a customer calls with an order requiring immediate delivery, you will check the inventory status on the computer. This will tell you what the quantity on hand of this item was as of the last time you ran the batch update. It may show inventory on hand when in fact that inventory had been sold this morning. In this case, the need for timely information overshadows the need for batch controls.

This is where on-line processing excels. In an on-line environment, each time you enter a transaction into your machine it updates your files immediately. This means that when you look at your stock status, you are seeing it as it exists as of the last transaction input. The advantage of this approach is mitigated somewhat by the natural tendency to let a bunch of transactions build up in the in-basket before going through the task of entering them. Due to the limited capacity of diskettes, you generally won't have more than one system up and running at a time. To change from inventory control to receivables means changing diskettes and running a different program. Systems with hard disks in the multi-megabyte range partially overcome this problem by having all the data files present on one disk and allowing several different programs to be run simultaneously (from different terminals). If it has been programmed to switch easily from one set of programs to another, you may not run into this problem.

The choice between on-line and batch applications depends a lot on what is being done. In the case of inventory, timeliness may be the deciding factor. For accounts payable, where you have to insert checks into the printer, the batch orientation is superior. Since on-line or batch processing is a function of how the individual program is written and not of the hardware or operating system, you can support both methods on the same machine with some of your applications being batch and some being on-line. Whichever you choose, or are forced into, be sure you've spent enough time practicing on the software in question so that you're comfortable with its procedures. Next to dissatisfaction with a system's outputs, I would say that unhappiness with a system's processing and inputting procedures causes the most failures in small business automation.

HUMAN ENGINEERING

This funny phrase refers to engineering *for* humans, not *of* humans. In general, a product has good human engineering when it is easy for a human to use. Did you ever try to tighten a bolt in a car that was in such a position that, even if you could reach it, there was no room in there for a socket wrench? Even if the placement of that bolt was a stroke of genius in terms of stress, load relief, chassis integrity, or what have you, it was not human-engineered. Sometimes a product meant only for use by humans ignores human engineering. Remember the ecologically-sound aluminum beer can top that opened your thumb at the same time you opened the beer? Or how about twist-off beer bottle tops that demonstrate the thin line between pain and pleasure?

The software you use should be primarily designed to service you, the user, and not just the machine or the programmer. Having written many thousands of lines of code myself, I know what a pain in the neck it is to human-engineer a program. It makes the program twice as long because it involves displaying clear, wordy, unmistakable prompts to the user — including lots of error-checking codes. This means trying to out-guess every potential user in the world and anticipate what foolish tricks they will try with the program. Not only does it take time, from the vendor's point of view, but it takes a lot of money to carry this human approach throughout a system.

A program that has been ideally written from a human engineering point of view will leave nothing to your imagination. The author will have assumed you know nothing except the basic operating procedures of your machine, such as how to turn it on, change disks, etc. The program will tell you quite explicitly what to do every step of the way. It will eliminate the need for you to refer repeatedly to the documentation or reference manuals provided with the software. It will edit your responses and not allow you to proceed until you give a correct one. To aid you in this process it will never ask an open-ended question but always give you a limited list of choices. No matter what key you strike at any time (with the exception of keys that communicate directly with the hardware, like break, escape, or reset), the program will be ready for it and will not abort with a program error. A truly sophisticated system will allow you to input "HELP" in response to any question and will in return display some explanation of what it is seeking. This is not as unusual as it sounds. I have worked on at least one system in the $15 thousand range that provided this feature, and it is becoming more and more commonplace.

One of the ideas behind the software-evaluation technique I discussed earlier in this chapter (see "How to Buy It") is to bring out the kinds of problems or pleasures a particular piece of software can offer by the way it was written, the prompts it displays, and the help it gives in correcting your errors. Growing sophistication among makers of software will eventually produce more or less standardized software packages, as the necessary and desirable features of any application are naturally selected out of the inferior products. The way in which these packages present themselves to you through the medium of the CRT and the ways they interact with you, guiding you through the steps they need to do their tasks, may very well ultimately decide which package you buy.

DOCUMENTATION

This is a very touchy subject with me. As a programmer, systems analyst, and finally a manager of commercial data processing departments, I have always believed in the value of good documentation. Turnover in the computer industry is so high that almost no one stays longer than 2 years on a job. This means that you are always moving into a job that someone else had half-completed or you are always leaving behind some system that either needed a lot of work or at least required maintenance. I grew to love everything about documentation. Wherever it existed, people were happy and productivity was high. Where is was absent or poorly organized, a crisis atmosphere prevailed.

When I switched from writing software for internal company use to writing software that was intended for many people of varying intelligence and technical competence, documentation took on a new meaning. The self-documenting aspects of a system — that is, the prompts and messages that come from the programs themselves — becomes the most important element in the documenting process. Second on this list is a reference manual.

In the process of selecting a software package for your business, you will be called upon to make a very complex decision based on information that may be at the frontiers of your comprehension. Documentation can make this job much easier. It should not only explain to you what the system does in such a way that you can easily understand, but it should also provide a yardstick by which you can measure the competence and professionalism of the writers of the system. All of the necessary items of documentation can be contained in the reference manual. The more of them in the following list that appear in a manual, the higher you should rate the system:

1. *The index.* I put this first because it is the roadmap to the documentation. One popular manufacturer tried to replace the index entirely with a comprehensive table of contents. It was an utter failure. Mail order indexes for the manual became a popular item among the owners of these systems.

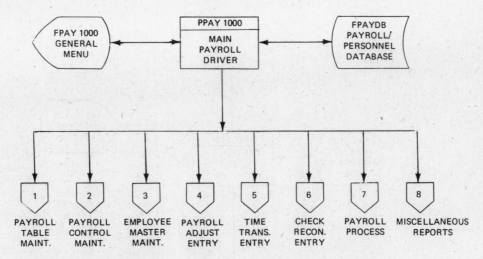

Figure 18. Overview of a payroll system. (Courtesy Collier–Jackson, Inc.)

You don't give a hoot about the table of contents. It's not the way you need the information presented. When you think of a subject that you need information on, you want to see alphabetical order as in an index, not page order as in a table of contents. By the time you've completed the test procedure for software selection, you'll have had to use the manual enough to know whether the index is any good.

2. *System overview.* The overview should explain briefly but clearly how the information flows through the system from program to program and from file to file. It should be presented both pictorially, in the form of systems flow charts as shown in Figures 18 and 19, and in narrative form. From the overview you should be able to see (1) all the files in the system, (2) which programs add to or change information in them, and (3) how they interact with each other.

The narrative portion should explain the purpose of the system, define its major components or subsystems, and describe the minimum hardware requirements to run the system. It should also include a section on the limits and capacities of the system.

Figure 18 shows a payroll program, named "PPAY1000," which displays a general menu and interacts with the payroll and personnel data, collectively known in this system as "FPAYDB." The menu displays 8 choices to the user. Selecting choice 1 transfers control from the main payroll program to the payroll table maintenance program. The symbols in Figures 18 and 19 containing the "1"s are called off-page connectors and help you follow the flow chart from one page to the next.

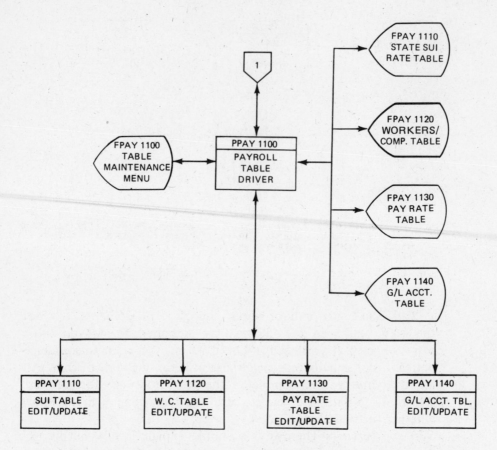

Figure 19. Subsystem within payroll. (Courtesy Collier–Jackson, Inc.)

In Figure 19 the payroll table maintenance program is shown displaying another menu that allows the user to select from among 4 different functions. At the end of these programs, control returns up the flow chart to the PPAY1100 program, and then to the PPAY1000 program.

3. *Procedures.* Procedures fall into two categories: how-to-do and what-to-do. The how-to's include such things as:

1. Powering up the system;
2. Entering and exiting from programs;
3. How to do backups;
4. The operation of any utilities;
5. How to line up the checks in the printer; and
6. How to perform preventive maintenance; etc.

What-to-do's tell you what you need to do in order to get the job done, tell you whether it is processing payroll, keep track of inventories, or run a general ledger. It should cover such topics as:

1. What files need to be built initially before bringing the system on line;
2. What programs need to be run in which sequence in order to complete the accounting cycle;
3. What files each program updates;
4. What the various prompts mean; and
5. What the choices are for reply.

Figure 20 shows an excellent procedure for printing payroll checks.

4. *Training.* One of the biggest complaints by dealers of small business systems in the $10 thousand–$30 thousand range is that the low margins make it unprofitable to do much handholding and training of the users. Systems of this size do not require that much less training than systems selling at twice or even three times their cost. Moreover, until the industry becomes aware of the need to emphasize training in the manual, dealers will never free themselves from the incessant questions pouring in from every user.

In this regard, I must give Radio Shack very high marks for its Scripsit® word processing program. Although for reference purposes the manual is almost worthless, the package comes with 6 hours of training in the form of audio-cassettes. You just slap them in a cassette player, sit down at your computer, and let the voice on the tape show you everything you need to know about the programs. By the time you finish the lessons, you hardly need to refer to the manual anymore. But generally, don't expect to find much in the way of training in the documentation. It's an idea whose time is just beginning.

5. *Screen layouts.* You may think that reproducing manually the screens that the computer displays for a given program would be trivial. After all, you can display them at will by running the program, can't you? However, if your documentation includes them, you will be referring to them repeatedly. They give a fast clue as to what information the program gathers from or displays to the user. Additionally, if they are documented in the manner shown in Figure 21, they give additional valuable information about the contents of each field on the screen. These descriptions are extremely useful in locating information needed while you are actually operating the system.

6. *Report layouts.* Again, you might ask, why document report layouts when you can run the report yourself? Well, first, you can match up the output of your data with the documentation to see if the program is operating correctly. Second, you can refer to these layouts to select the report that will give the infor-

9.01 CHECK WRITER RUN PROCEDURES

Program PPAY0410 (the standard check print program) is designed to be run with an on-line printer to insure proper control of checks written and void. Operator assistance is required through a number of console responses.

When PPAY0410 begins to execute, it displays to the systems console the following:

```
BEGIN CHECK PRINT RUN
ENTER     =LIMIT 0
ENTER     =OUTFENCE 13
ENTER     =SPOOL 6,STOP
ENTER     =HEADOFF6
MOUNT CHECK FORM ON PRINTER
WHEN CHECKS ARE READY RESPOND "GO"
TO TERMINATE THIS RUN RESPOND "STOP"
AWAITING REPLY (MAX. CHARS. = 18)?
```

At this point follow the instructions as displayed by the program with the "GO" response last. Leave the standard forms in the printer until the program prints the first line-up check, then remove the paper and place the check forms in. While inserting the check forms, the program will have displayed on the console:

```
TO GET ANOTHER ALIGN CHECK, RESPOND "NEXT"
TO BEGIN PRINTING CHECK, RESPOND "GO"
TO TERMINATE THIS RUN, RESPOND "STOP"
AWAITING REPLY, (MAX. CHAR. = 18)?
```

You can continue to enter "NEXT" until you are satisfied with the line-up. A "GO" reply will cause the program to display:

```
ENTER NUMBER OF FIRST CHECK (6 DIGITS)
AWAITING REPLY, (MAX. CHAR. = 18)?
```

Open the printer to check what the next available check number is and respond to the request. The program will then display:

```
IS THIS A RESTART -- YES OR NO
AWAITING REPLY, (MAX. CHARS. = 18)?
```

A "NO" reply will cause the system to begin printing check immediately. A "YES" reply will cause the system to display:

```
ENTER RESTART KEY
COMPANY DIVISION DEPARTMENT EMPLOYEE NO.
IF DIVISION AND/OR DEPARTMENT ARE NOT PRESENT
--- ENTER SPACES
AWAITING REPLY (MAX. CHARS. = 18)?
```

Figure 20. What you should expect from procedures documentation. (Courtesy Collier-Jackson, Inc.)

```
                                     OPERATION INSTRUCTIONS
                                  CHECK WRITER RUN PROCEDURES



At this point enter the COMPANY DIVISION DEPARTMENT EMPLOYEE
NUMBER of the employee you wish to begin reprinting checks.
Format is XXYYZZZ70123456789.

The system will then display:

          ENTER LAST EMPLOYEE PRINTED
          ENTER EVEN IF ITS THE SAME AS THE RESTAART KEY
          COMPANY DIVISION DEPARTMENT EMPLOYEE NO.
          IF DIVISION AND/OR DEPARTMENT ARE NOT PRESENT
          -- ENTER SPAACES
          AWAITING REPLY, (MAX. CHARS. = 18)?

This reply is required if your company is using the system check
reconciliation.  By entering the last employee's check printed,
the range is given to the program so that check recon records
generated for these people can be voided.  If check recon is not
use, this reply should be indentical to the restart key.

Upon completion of check printing the system will display:

          END OF CHECK PRINT RUN
          REMOUNT STANDARD FORMS ON PRINTER
          ENTER    =SPOOL6,STARTOUT
          ENTER    =HEADON6
          RESET    =OUTFENCE TO NORMAL VALUE
          RESET    =LIMIT TO NORMAL VALUE
          WHEN FORMS READY, RESPOND "GO"
          AWAITING REPLY, (MAX. CHARS. = 18)?

Follow the above instruction, replying "GO" last. At this point
the spooler has been turned on and normal processing continues.
```

Figure 20 continued.

mation you are seeking without running them all to see what's on them. Third, and most important, if they are documented in the manner shown in Figure 22, you will learn something about what each of the fields on the report means.

7. *Program narrative.* You might think that knowing how a given program actually operates would be unnecessary. However, you will almost certainly have occasion to ask both of the following questions sometime during the operation of your system: (1) Does this program update a certain file, or not? and (2) How does this program calculate a certain value (like aging receivables, sales tax calculation, or overtime pay, etc.)? The program nar-

```
                        OFF-LINE REPORTING MENU

        (1)  SELECTION  □   (2)  PAY PERIOD (IF OTHER THAN CURRENT)  □□

***** PAYROLL TABLE REPORTS *****        ******* PERSONNEL REPORTS *******
1  STATE INSURANCE TABLE                 6   EMPLOYEE STATUS NOTICES
2  WORKERS' COMPENSATION TABLE           7   EMPLOYEE SUMMARY
3  PAY RATE TABLE                        8   EEO-1 SECTION D
4  GENERAL LEDGER ACCOUNT TABLE          9   EMPLOYEE HISTORY
5  DEDUCTION TABLE


            *************** OTHER ***************
            A  TIME TRANSACTIONS EDIT
            B  ADJUSTMENT TRANSACTIONS EDIT
            C  WORKER'S COMPENSATION REPORT
            D  DEDUCTION RECAP REPORT
            F  PRINT BLANK EMPLOYEE STATUS NOTICES
                 (insert number desired in pay period box above)

     (3)    J  OTHER JOB NAME  _____

            E  EXIT
```

OFF-LINE REPORTING MENU
(#1,800)

The Off-Line Reporting Menu provides the user with reports from the Control Table Reports and the Personnel Reports. The user also has the option of selecting another job other then the report selections offered on the screen by selecting a job within the established job group.

FIELD NUMBER & NAME	ENTRY REQUIREMENTS
1 SELECTION	The user selects the report desired from the available options offered on the screen.
2 PAY PERIOD (PAY-PERIOD-NO)	This field is entered by the user if any other then the current period is to be affected.
3 OTHER JOB NAME	The user has the option of selecting any of the other jobs available within the established job group.

Figure 21. Screen layout with descriptive material. (Courtesy Collier–Jackson, Inc.)

LOS ALTOS, CA 94022
INVENTORY STATUS REPORT

CLASS CODE: 0
BULK STOCK

PART NUMBER	DESCRIPTION	UM	SC	QUANTITY ON HAND	QUANT ON ORDER	QUANT IN PROC	QUANT SHORT	DATE LAST TRANS	LST 1 DAYS USAGE	LST 2 MONTHS USAGE	UNIT COST	EXTENDED COST
100-1	SALT	02	B	135	100	0	11	10/02/78	23	0	1.087	146.687
100-11	PAPER TOWELS	FT	B	1000	0	0	0	8/24/78	0	0	.040	40.000
100-2	PEPPER	EA	B	238	500	0	13	7/29/78	0	0	.320	76.160
100-3	GARLIC SALT	EA	B	135	0	0	0	7/29/78	0	0	2.500	337.500
100-5	FRYING PAN 16"	EA	B	1	0	0	0	7/29/78	0	0	9.600	9.600
100-6	SPATULA	EA	B	2	0	0	0	7/29/78	0	0	3.200	6.400
100-7	BOWL, 6"	EA	B	3	12	0	7	7/29/78	0	0	2.300	6.900
100-8	SPONGE, SYNTHETHIC	EA	B	2	0	0	0	7/29/78	0	0	.570	1.140
100-9	SOAP	BR	B	4	0	0	0	7/29/78	0	0	.350	1.400

TOTAL EXTENDED COST: 625.787

(1) (2) (3) (4) (5) (6) (7) (8) (9) (10) (11) (12) (13)

Figure 22. A well documented report layout. (Courtesy ASK Computer Systems, Inc.)

RE, 100: INVENTORY STATUS REPORT

COL. REF.	TITLE	EXPLANATION
1	PART NUMBER	Unique item number associated with a part.
2	DESCRIPTION	Full 30-character description of the part.
3	UM	Part's unit of measure: EA = each, LB = pounds, etc.
4	SC	Source code: M = Part is made in-house. B = Part is purchased from an outside vendor. S = Part is subcontracted to an outside vendor. X = Blow-through R = Routable sub-assembly F = Free stock
5	QUANT ON HAND	Number of parts in stock.
6	QUANT ON ORDER	Number of parts, not yet issued to stock, on open purchase orders.
7	QUANT IN PROC	Number of parts, not yet issued to stock, on open work orders.
8	QUANT SHORT	Total recorded kit shortages for this part.
9	DATE LAST TRANS	Date of the last transaction that changed the quantity on hand balance of this part.
10	LST N DAYS USAGE	Part's usage (issues from stock) since the beginning of the month.

11	LST M MONTHS USAGE	Part's usage in the last M months. M is user defined.
12	UNIT COST	Part's unit cost. This depends upon the costing flag, the cost center, and the source code. (See Methods of Costing in the appendix for further information).
13	EXTENDED COST	A part's extended cost equals QOH × Unit Cost.

AD, 400: ADDING A NEW PURCHASE ORDER

This command requires the following information for each purchase order: PURCHASE ORDER NUMBER, BUYER CODE, and VENDOR CODE. The following information is required for each line item on a purchase order: PART NUMBER, UNIT COST, QUANTITY, VENDOR PROMISED DATE, and DELIVERY DATE.

If the UNIT COST entered is outside of a user specified variance limit (COMIN variable 19) with the Material Cost on file for a part, a WARNING message stating the standard material cost on file is printed and the user is given the opportunity to continue input for this part.

MANMAN allows multiple delivery schedules for any part on a purchase order. Entering carriage RETURN in response to the prompt 'PART NUMBER?' will be understood by MANMAN to mean that the user is entering another delivery date for the same part.

If the user has selected the option to use MFGFIL (COMIN variable 89), then this command will list all potential source part numbers for the part being ordered and will request the specific source for this particular P. O.

When all parts are entered on a purchase order, the user should respond to the 'PART NUMBER?' prompt with an *END*. This will cause MANMAN to prompt with 'PURCHASE ORDER NUMBER?' and the user is ready to enter the next purchase order or 'END' to return to MANMAN command level.

Figure 23. Program narrative. (Courtesy ASK Computer Systems, Inc.)

rative should answer both of these questions by including both the files updated and any algorithms the program uses in calculating values for storage or reporting. Additionally, the narrative should explain briefly the purpose of the program and how it functions. (See Figure 23.)

8. *Record layouts.* In order to understand record layouts, three terms need definition: field, record, and file. A field is one item of information (within a record). A record is a collection of several logically related fields, each of which is identical in format (i.e., the same fields of the same size in the same order appear in each record). All the records together form a file.

A telephone book is a good example of this scheme. Each entry in the book is the equivalent of a record. Each record is made up of the same fields — last name, first name, address, and telephone number — although the information in each of the corresponding fields of the records will be different. All the records or entries together is a file of all names, addresses, and telephone numbers — the telephone directory.

Record layouts describe each field in the record. It should give its symbolic name, the one used in the program to refer to it, a description of the field, its length in bytes, what its form is (alphabetic, numeric, or numeric with decimal point, etc.), and, in some cases, the allowable values this field can take on. Generally, you will have very little real need for these layouts unless you are the adventurous type who would rather alter the contents of a record and all the programs that access this record than adjust yourself and your business to the way the system was written. Even so, there is something mysteriously gratifying in being able to look at these layouts. They seem to raise one's level of comprehension of what the system is doing and how it does it, even though one never actually operates on this information. Perhaps it's the "picture worth a thousand words" phenomenon.

Documentation, more than any other factor, determines how easily you will be able to learn and operate your software. Any time spent reading boring manuals before buying will pay off handsomely in the end.

A SIMPLE SYSTEM — INVENTORY

In order to enhance your understanding of the descriptions of the rather complex applications systems to be presented in the next chapter, let's study for a few minutes an oversimplified version of an inventory system. Using the primal system idea described earlier, we must answer four questions:

1. What do we want to store for retrieval, inspection, updating, etc.?
2. What inputs are required to mimic this real-life activity in the computer?
3. What output do we want from the system?
4. What does the real-life process look like (in flow chart form) and how will the programs operate?

Storage. For each part of your inventory, we will create one record on the inventory file contained on your disk (or diskette). This record will contain only two pieces of information: the part number and the current quantity in stock. This quantity will be increased by receipts from your suppliers and decreased by sales to your customers (or issues to your production process).

Input. For each transaction, we need to input to the computer three pieces of data: the part number, the quantity, and whether the transaction is a sale (an issue from inventory) or a receipt.

Process. We will need three programs to accomplish all of these activities. Together, they will constitute your inventory system. One program lets you input your changes to inventory. A second program will ask you for a part number, fetch the record from the file containing the part number and its associated quantity on hand, and display it on the terminal. A third program will sort the file by part number and will print on your line printer, line by line, the part number and quantity, giving you a report of stock status as it exists at the time the program is run. It is patterned after your manual inventory system, and if you key in the proper part number and quantity each time and each issue or receipt at the time it occurs, inventory quantities in the file will accurately reflect what is in stock.

Output. What we want displayed at any time is either the current quantity of a given inventory item (which will display on the CRT) or a listing of the complete inventory by part number, showing the current quantity in stock for each item.

ANOTHER SIMPLE SYSTEM — THE SALES JOURNAL

Another handy function to put in your computer is the sales journal, which will tell you how much of each product you have sold to each customer and when. (See Figure 25.)

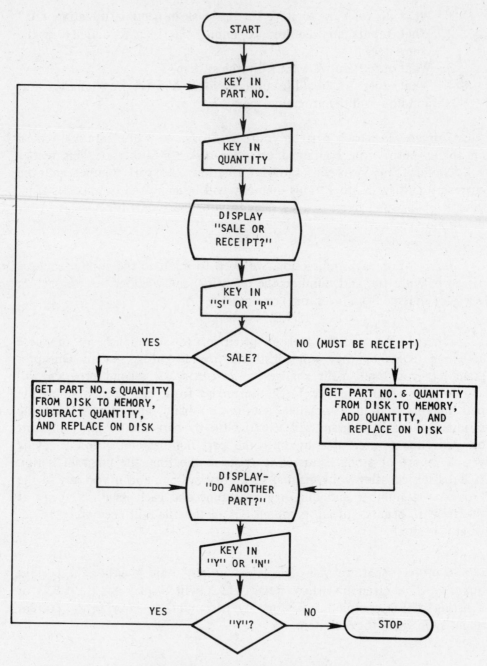

Figure 24. A simple inventory system.

Storage. This time we will use two files. The first file will have one record for each customer. Each record will contain the customer name or number and the total dollar amount sold to this customer to date. The second file will contain one record for each sale. The record will consist

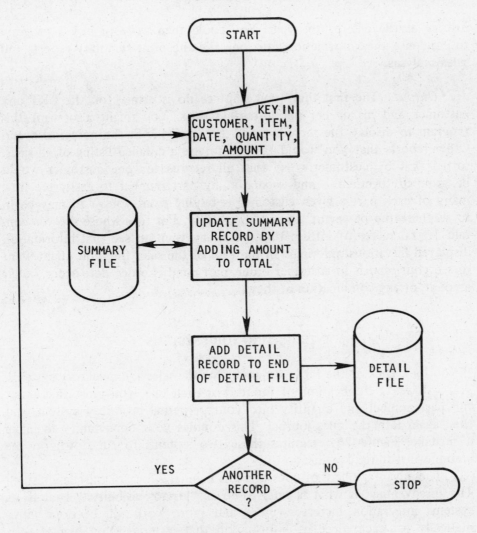

Figure 25. The sales journal.

of the customer name or number, the date of sale, the item or items sold, the quantity sold, and the dollar amount of the sale. The first file is a summary file. The second file is a detail file.

Input. In this case, the inputs for each transaction are customer, item sold, date, quantity, and dollar amount.

Process. The flowchart for the input program is shown in Figure 25. To complete the system, you will need additional programs for the reports you want to generate and for the CRT retrievals and displays you want. You also need a program to zero out the amount fields at the end of each month or year. If you make a copy of the files at the end of each month before zeroing out the fields, you could assemble a complete sales history at the end of the year. You could then write or buy a program to condense this information into one file and print summary reports and sales analyses.

Output. The first thing you want to do is display on the CRT any customer and his or her period-to-date sales. You might also want this program to display the records from the detail file in chronological order. Other reports that you would find useful are a detailed listing of all sales, sorted first by customer — so that all records for one customer would be grouped together — and secondly, by part number to easily see how many of each part a given customer is buying from you. You may begin to see here the power of a good sort utility. For files whose records contain several pieces of information, you may want to see that information displayed in various orderings. In the case of the sales file, you might want to see your reports in customer order, part number order, date order, dollar amount, or any combination of these.

INTEGRATING YOUR SYSTEMS

If you look back at the input programs for the sales and inventory systems, you will see a duplication of input. For each sale, you must first input the part number and quantity into your perpetual inventory system, and then again into the sales journal. This doubles your opportunity to make a mistake. Figure 26 integrates these two systems to cut down on the amount of required key-ins.

The advantage here of course is less manual effort for the same results. The disadvantage is what is referred to as "loss of visibility." That is, as systems integration increases, more and more work will be done automatically for each piece of information that is input. You won't see it happen each time as you did in the previous case, where the information was input twice. If it goes in correctly the first time, you eliminate the possibility for errors occurring on subsequent inputs to other systems. If it goes in wrong, it will mess up every file it touches.

So the level of integration of your applications depends on (1) your need to have data files from different applications on-line concurrently, (2) your need for more than one terminal, and (3) the amount of money you need or want to invest.

FULL INTEGRATION

Figure 27 is a diagram of a fully integrated manufacturing/financial system. As shown, the systems interact with a minimum of input. It is still

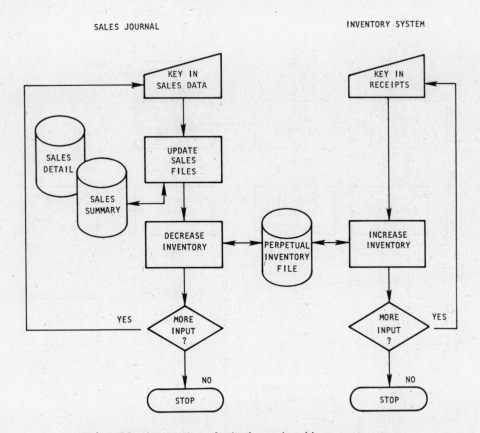

SALES JOURNAL   INVENTORY SYSTEM

Figure 26. Integration of sales journal and inventory systems.

necessary to key in sales, purchase orders, receipt of goods, receipt of cash, and payment of bills. Sales inputs will automatically generate order entry paperwork (invoice, sales order, shipper, packing list, etc.), an entry to accounts receivable, possibly an order to manufacturing, and an update to inventory. Cash in or out will affect payables or receivables, which in turn will affect the general ledger. Material from suppliers increases the quantities on hand and decreases the open order files in the purchasing system. Movement to manufacturing decreases raw materials inventory and may generate purchase orders at predetermined order levels.

The MRP (Materials Requirements Planning) system uses a forecast of sales over time, the current raw materials inventory, what is in finished goods, and what is on order in the purchasing system, to create time-sequenced production schedules and buy requirements.

This level of sophistication in systems integration is not yet available on microprocessor-based systems. Not that the hardware can't handle it; it could very easily. It's just that the software has yet to be written. (It does exist in pieces, however.)

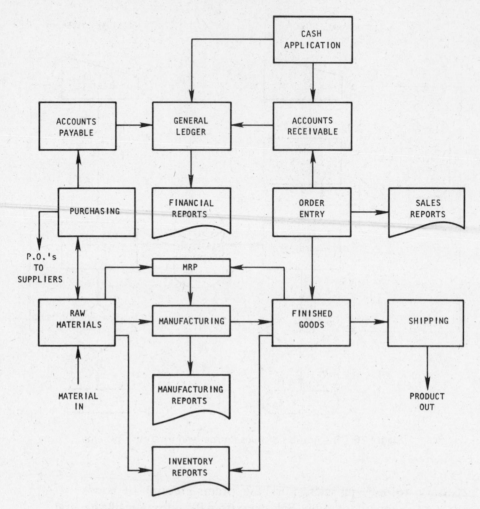

Figure 27. Integrated manufacturing/financial system.

Just as you can begin with a small computer system and expand the hardware in modules, so software can be designed to be implemented in modules, expanding the capabilities of your system. This approach gives immediate benefits from your system without having to implement the full-blown applications network.

There are two things, then, that you should look for when evaluating a particular vendor's software with respect to integration. First, what integration or links, if any, exist between the various packages being offered? If they are minimal, find out how, for example, you will get all of your subsidiary ledgers — i.e., sales, receivables, payables, and payroll — posted to the general ledger. Second, if the level of integration is considerable, this implies that the data for several systems need to be on-line or present on the disk or diskette at the same time. This increases the requirements for storage and may mean dual density or dual-sided diskettes, or even a hard disk drive (very expensive).

MAKE OR BUY

Early in your computerization process, you will be faced with the question of buying prewritten applications programs from a software company or writing it yourself (meaning hiring someone to design and program your applications for you). As the quantity of preprogrammed software expands, the greater are your chances of finding a suitable package for your system. There is no point in re-inventing the wheel. For standard applications like payroll, accounts receivable, inventory control, etc., try to find software that has already been written and tested and has a track record of success. If your business has unique requirements, you will have to have some software written, or at least modified, to suit you. This process of obtaining custom software is one of the trickiest and most hazardous things you can do. The following case histories are some examples of what can happen. (Adapted from Tom McCusker, "The Hazards and Rewards of Creating Your Own Programs," *ACU Newsletter,* Small Computer Section, Volume 1, Number 3, June 1980, with permission.)

Case 1

Jerome Garfield wanted to automate the manual system for his mortgage service company. He purchased an IBM 5110 for $12 thousand to do this. However, after 1 year of trying to program his system to do the things his company did manually, Garfield got "fed up with the whole thing." During that year, he also spent $10 thousand on programming fees to implement a system that he ended up not using.

There are many vendors who offer packages with their systems. It often appears that these systems can do everything you need done — general ledger, accounts receivable and payable, inventory control, and even transaction processing of orders and invoices. Once installed, however, you'll often find that you must completely alter the way you've operated manually. Customizing the program itself can be complicated and costly, and IBM admits that only 20 to 50% of its customers are able to use the new 5120 as is.

Most consultants advise small businesses to avoid having to customize their programs by being explicit when purchasing the computer. Dealing with a vendor who can meet your particular specifications can save lots of programming time.

Case 2

Bob Tuffias needed a computer to help manage a fast growing company that supplied macrame goods to retailers. He decided on an IBM 5110 and contracted a company called Ven-Data to install the packages he needed to put the computer in operation. He later bought a package called BRADS II, put out by IBM. This enabled him to manipulate files and predict production needs on a weekly basis.

Tuffias is satisfied with the system, but admits it was a lengthy and expensive undertaking. His initial purchase cost was $12 thousand in 1978, and customizing the package to meet his company's needs totaled $30 thousand. Carol John, owner of Ven-Data, believes that more than half of the purchasers of the IBM 5120 will have to have additional customizing done on their programs. For example, an order entry package that is available does not generate packing slips. "And there is nothing in the package to let you know you're out of stock."

Case 3

Robert L. Hallock of E. S. Products, Inc., bought an IBM model 5110 in 1978. After 2 years the computer was still not going to be operational until the following September. Hallock turned to a programming house in New York — Software Design Associates — for help. After a few months, the programming company informed him that it could not do the job at the originally quoted price. Eventually, E. S. hired a freelance programmer, John N. Carielli, to work on the computer system.

Hallock's experience was a simple case of a vendor not learning the applications needs of the customer. Hardware features are often over-emphasized by a vendor, leaving many small businesses with a system that's difficult and costly to implement. In addition, temporary help may have to be sought to convert the new system, often costing more than expected. This type of case can happen in multimillion dollar corporations as well as in small businesses.

Case 4

Photo Engineering Corp. of Los Angeles is a nationwide supplier of photographs of newborn babies. It acquired a Basic Four small business computer for $38 thousand in 1973. After 2 years of installation, the system was worth $112 thousand. Says Marc Arnold, who developed some of the in-house programs for Photo Engineering, "Sure, you could shop around for packages which a system house can modify; but in more and more cases, we find that we can best design them from scratch."

Case 5

Because of the uniqueness of its business, Chandler Lumber Co., one of California's largest lumber wholesalers, decided to develop its own software. It was essential that the package have an automatic lumber estimating system. A system was developed, but found to be too primitive. Jim McCarthy, head of the data processing staff for Chandler, said that because lumber prices change almost weekly, the company had to be able to take future pricing trends into consideration when quoting prices to its customers. As a result, McCarthy developed its own package with the help of a consultant. It also replaced a Microdata "Reality" computer, which it had outgrown, for a Honeywell Level 6 system. In other words, Chandler Lumber found that the cheapest way to develop the lumber estimating program was to do it themselves.

Case 6

Art Szerlip Sales Co., of Van Nuys, California, is a relatively small electronic manufacturer. It installed its first computer — an ADAM, made by Logical Machine Corp. of Sunnyvale, California — in 1977. It has since developed its own programs to do inventory control, invoicing, sales analysis listings, sales personnel control, open commission reporting, and mailing lists. All of these functions had been done manually in the past, except for historical sales analysis, which was done through a computer service bureau.

President Art Szerlip now provides over 125 programs for his firm, at an estimated cost of about $30 thousand. Szerlip found a way to make the computer bend to the way he did business, instead of the other way around. "And there's nothing too mysterious about computers. The average person with a little bit of smarts could be qualified to build his own programs after playing for 20 to 40 hours on the keyboard," says Szerlip.

Of course, you may not have the time to experiment with computer programming. One alternative to paying expensive consulting fees, in this case, may be to look at colleges and universities. Many educational institutes offer programming assistance from their students and faculty at rates considerably lower than those offered by private firms. An example of this is a project in which student teams define the needs of a particular small business. Under the supervision of a faculty advisor, they then draw up specifications for a computer system. One company that used such a service even ended up hiring one of the student programmers from the project full time.

One thing is certain: As the small business computer industry increases and matures, vendors will become more and more aware of the problems in developing software. In the next 10 years, the small business computer market will reach $7 billion, with another $5 billion in associated program package sales. As these numbers are approached, packages will be so tailored to specific small businesses. As a result, the computer itself will be a secondary factor in automating, and it will be the package, and not the computer, that will be sold.

5

APPLICATIONS
SOFTWARE – SOME
SPECIFIC SYSTEMS

This chapter will explain what each of the most popular small business systems – namely accounts receivable, accounts payable, general ledger, order entry, inventory control, purchasing, and payroll – are supposed to do in a computer system. Figure 28 shows how these systems compare in popularity among current users and future users. It is interesting to note that accounts receivable is being used by twice as many current users as inventory control; among possible purchasers, inventory control has a marked edge over all the other applications.

To describe these systems I will again use the primal system approach, identifying what the output from each of them should be, what elements are to be stored, what inputs you will be required to provide, and what various processes these systems should perform for you.

HOW TO READ THE RECORD LAYOUTS

I have greatly simplified the record layouts. The length of the various fields will vary from one system to another, as will the form of the numeric fields (those fields for which only numbers are "legal", like quantity on hand or unit price). Therefore, specifying length and/or type might be misleading. Likewise, the symbolic names of the fields will vary.

For example, the part number field for an inventory control system might have the symbolic name PN in one system, PART in another, and PARTNO in yet another. Since the names of these fields will definitely vary from one program to another, they are not relevant to a presentation of a generalized system.

Basically, what we find on the record layout is the description and three other specifications, which appear to the left of the description.

Current Users	*Pct.* *	*Possible Purchasers*	*Pct.* **
Accounts Receivable	51	Inventory Control	42
Accounts Payable	45	Accounts Receivable	34
Payroll	40	Accounts Payable	28
General Ledger	26	Payroll	23
Inventory Control	26	Billing	15
Billing	23	General Ledger	14
Purchasing	15	Purchasing	10
Order Entry	8	Cost Accounting	8
Cost Accounting	7		
Sales Analysis	6		

*Three most important applica-
tions named, weighted equally.

**Two most important
applications named, weighted
equally.

Projected Universe: 1,711,357 small businesses in industries with the highest potential for computer utilization.

Figure 28. Most frequently mentioned computer applications in small businesses. (Courtesy Time, Inc.)

(See Figure 29.) The first of these is the optional field indicator. Those data items I consider to be absolutely essential to the record have no asterisk in this column. Systems that do not include these essential items should be very carefully evaluated to see if they can still do the job. An asterisk in this field indicates that the data item is considered optional.

Next to the optional indicator is the key indicator. An asterisk in this position indicates that the whole record should be retrievable by specifying the value in this key field. For example, in the sales order entry system, you obviously would want to look at a sales order based on the sales order number, just as you do in a manual system. The automated system should allow you to specify the sales order number as a key and retrieve the whole sales order based on that information. This implies that the key, in this case, the sales order number, is unique. If a different sales order with the same number were entered, the operating system that takes care of the storage and retrieval of data records should not accept it. Some sort of message indicating a duplicate key should appear on the screen. Any operating system that allows you to write over an existing record with an identical key, without asking you first, should be rejected without further consideration. You can check for this condition by trying the software before buying it.

Some record layouts may have more than one key field. Sometimes two fields are concatenated; that is, strung together likethesefourwords,

OPT	KEY	LINK	DESCRIPTION
	*		Invoice number
		*	Bill-to-customer
*		*	Ship-to-customer
			Invoice date
			Amount of invoice
			Cash applied
			Discount taken
*		*	Sales order number
*			Ship date
*			Date of last payment
*			Bill of lading number
*			Shipped via
*			Freight charges
*			Tax charges
*			Payment terms code

Figure 29. Invoice master file.

to form the key. In the case of accounts receivable detail file, the combination of the invoice number and line item number produce a unique key. For example, invoice number I82355 has three line items. You want to be able to store and retrieve each line item separately. The problem, since they all belong to invoice number I82355, is to create a unique identifier or key (remember, duplicate keys are not allowed). By concatenating the line item number with the invoice number, the unique keys are created — I823551, I823552, and I823553. When this is the case on the record layout, the two fields are joined by a bracket.

Some records will have multiple keys. This allows you to retrieve a given record in more than one way. For example, in the accounts payable system you may want the program to retrieve a record for you while your vendor is on the phone — a great argument settler. Looking at Figure 37 on page 101, you see that there are three keys and, hence, three ways you can get this particular transaction out of the files. If you know the voucher number, you can retrieve the record by specifying that value. If you don't know the voucher number, you are probably looking at the purchase order and can retrieve it that way. Finally, you could ask the vendor for his or her invoice number and get the information out that way.

Access methods that will support multiple keys in the same record are highly desirable. They allow more efficient and compact programs to be written.

Remember, all random access files require at least one key, a value that you can specify to the system to retrieve the record you want. When evaluating a system, determine which fields are the key fields for the various files. They should be logical selections based on the way you would normally ask to retrieve some piece of information in a manual system.

Finally, next to the key indicator is the link indicator. This is a handy way of indicating which fields in a record can serve as the key to retrieve a record from another file (for example, the accounts receivable master file record, complete with the name and address of the customer to whom the bill was sent.) After you input the invoice number, which is the master key to the invoice file, the program will retrieve the record whose number matched the number you input. However, before displaying the information, it would extract the bill-to-customer number from the record and use it as a key to retrieve the bill-to-customer record. Then it would be able to display the name and address of the customer along with the other invoice information.

ACCOUNTS RECEIVABLE SYSTEM

Accounting was one of the first areas taken over by computers in the bad old days of data processing — and for very good reasons. It is a painstaking, repetitive task, requiring absolute accuracy. It affects both the cash in and cash out of your company, and hence, timeliness is critical. There is no accounting task that you can do that is more important than accounts receivable. In my mind, it forms the nucleus of any computerized accounting system.

Integrated systems flow charts and block diagrams may show the general ledger at the physical center, and in fact, all data generally flow in that direction. But the general ledger is just a reporting device and as such is nowhere near as critical as your accounts receivable, the focal point of the financial health of your company. Since it has such a material effect on the welfare of your company, it is important for you to understand how this system should work on a computer and what you should expect from it.

Storage. A well-designed accounts receivable system will have at least three files associated with it: the invoice master file, the invoice detail file, and the customer master file, which I call the bill-to-customer master. (See Figures 29, 30, and 31.) I have also identified two optional files: the ship-to-customer master and the cash receipts file (see Figures 32 and 33), which will not be absolutely necessary to a good accounts receivable system but will enhance its utility considerably.

The *invoice master file* (see Figure 29) is keyed by invoice number, since this is the item unique to each invoice. It also has a field for the bill-to-customer number, which can be used as a key to retrieve the bill-to-

OPT	KEY	LINK	DESCRIPTION
{ *	*		Invoice number
{ *			Line item (from S.O.)
			Quantity
			Unit price
		*	Part number
*			Description
*			Unit cost
*			G/L sales account
*			G/L cost of sales account
*			Posting flag

Figure 30. Invoice detail file.

OPT	KEY	LINK	DESCRIPTION
	*		Bill-to-customer number
			Bill-to-name
			Bill-to-address line 1
			Bill-to-address line 2
*			Bill-to-address line 3
			Bill-to-city, state
			Bill-to-zip
			Credit limit
*			Telephone number
*			High balance
*			Current balance
*			Month-to-date sales booked
*			Month-to-date sales shipped
*			Month-to-date cost of sales
*			Year-to-date sales booked
*			Year-to-date sales shipped
*			Year-to-date cost of sales

Figure 31. Bill-to-customer master file.

customer information. (See Figure 31.) Some primitive systems include the customer name and address right in the invoice master record. This is extremely wasteful of disk storage space, since the entire name and address will be duplicated many times — once for each outstanding invoice for a given customer. With a customer master file and numbering scheme, only the customer number appears in the invoice master record, saving a lot of storage space.

An optional field, depending of course on the presence of the optional

OPT	KEY	LINK	DESCRIPTION
	*		Ship-to-customer number
*		*	Bill-to-customer number
			Ship-to-name
			Ship-to-address line 1
			Ship-to-address line 2
*			Ship-to-address line 3
			Ship-to-city, state
			Ship-to-zip
*			Telephone number

Figure 32. Ship-to-customer master file.

OPT	KEY	LINK	DESCRIPTION
	*	*	Invoice number
			Date of cash receipt
			Amount of cash receipt

Figure 33. Cash receipts file.

ship-to-customer file, is the ship-to-customer number. The importance of the amount of the invoice is self-evident.

The invoice date is essential because it provides the basis for your aged accounts receivable report. Having timely and accurate aged receivables reports is one of the most important reasons for automating your receivables. The cash-applied field will contain the to-date cash received on this invoice. The presence of a cash receipts file does diminish the importance of this data item. However, without this field the program would have to search through the cash receipts file for all the occurrences of this invoice number (the key to the cash receipts file) and add up all the amounts found therein. Having it present in the invoice master file speeds up processing of reports considerably. This can be particularly important if you want fast retrieval of this information on the CRT.

Access to data in the discount-taken field is important for two reasons. First, you will need it in order to balance the amounts billed with the amounts of cash received, and to post the same to the general ledger. Second, it gives you a way to analyze your credit policy. Easing of your credit policy should result in a drop in discounts taken and vice versa. If the programs are present to compare and report discounts taken from one period to the next, you'll have a very useful tool with which to monitor your credit policies.

If you have a sales order entry system that is integrated with your accounts receivable, the sales order number will provide a link to the sales order master file, enabling you to retrieve the original sales order by specifying only the invoice number. (Pretty handy, huh? The reverse should also be true.) For example, you enter I82355 as a key to retrieve the invoice record of the same number. When this is done, all the data in the fields in this record that are in memory are available for display on the screen, printing on a report, or whatever. The sales order number can now be removed from the record by the program and used as a key to retrieve the original sales order from the sales order entry master file. (See Figure 34.)

The date of last payment is a real argument settler. Having it at your fingertips can save you a lot of headaches and cause some to others. The ship date may appear in the sales order system; if so, it is unnecessary (and bad systems design) to have it appear again in the invoice master.

The bill of lading number, the date shipped, and the "shipped via" fields can be very useful if traffic is a major problem in your business.

The freight and tax charges border on being required fields. They should be included whenever an integrated general ledger is present, so that these amounts can be posted. In the absence of these fields, you can always enter tax and freight as line items in the invoice detail file. This is wasteful of storage, but it's better than not having them in the system at all.

Finally, I have seen payment terms appear both as a character field and as a coded field. If it is character, it appears written out (i.e., 2%, 10 days, net 30 days) and its usefulness is limited to being printed on the invoice. In code form, each of the different payment terms is assigned a code: "2%, 10 days, net 30 days" might be assigned to value 1; "Net 7" might have the value 2; 3 might signify "no discount," and so on. The more flexible systems will allow you to define your own terms and codes; less flexible systems will have them predetermined. Not only does this save storage space, but the codes can be used in analysis programs to yield reports concerning the terms given. In any case, having the field there at cash receipt time will prevent you from giving discounts not earned. (Of course, this implies that the program was written to check for this sort of thing.)

The *invoice detail file* contains one record for each line item ordered and shipped on a particular invoice. (See Figure 30 on page 89.) Using this master/detail scheme means that the master record does not have to be set up to contain a predefined, maximum number of detail items, as it would

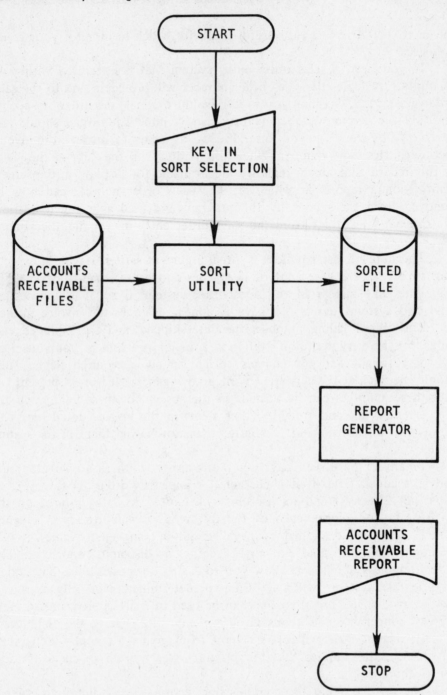

Figure 34.   A sort and report scheme.

if there were no detail record. This would place an arbitrary and restrictive limit on the number of items you could put on an invoice and would be extremely wasteful of disk space since each field defined in a record takes up the space allocated to it, whether that field contains data or not.

The master record can be linked to any number of detail records by using the invoice number concatenated to the line item number to produce a unique key. The required information in this file is the quantity, unit price, and part number. If the inventory system is present, this part number should link to the item master so that the description can be pulled out for reporting purposes. If not, you may find a description line in the detail file. Having the item master file on-line also eliminates the need to have the unit cost field in the invoice detail. The presence of the general ledger account fields allows you to break up your product lines into sub-ledgers for sales and cost of sales for reporting on the general ledger. When the amount of the line item is transferred to the general ledger, the posting flag is set to reflect this and to prevent double posting.

The *bill-to name and address file* is self-explanatory. I have made the credit limit field mandatory in this idealized system. This item, together with the high and current balance, can be combined into an extremely useful screen retrieval for on-the-spot credit checking and approval. The month-to-date and year-to-date fields provide a means for sales analysis by customer, backlog reporting (booked minus shipped), and gross margin calculation. These features are extremely desirable and reflect a high degree of awareness on the part of the systems designers.

There are two additional files that greatly enhance the utility of an accounts receivable system. The first is the cash receipts file. It is keyed by invoice number, which also links to the invoice master and detail files. It contains only the date of receipt and the amount. Having this file makes it easy to trace the payment history of a customer on a given invoice or all invoices for a customer.

The second file, the ship-to-name-and-address file, is particularly handy if there is a program to print shipping documents on your preprinted forms.

Outputs. As in all the systems presented in this chapter, the outputs from your accounts receivable system fall into two categories: printed reports and screen retrievals. The value of a powerful sort utility will become obvious when we discuss reports. A well-designed system will generate all reports with the general method shown in the flow chart in Figure 34. Under this scheme, you specify which data item(s) you would like to see the report sorted by (i.e., customer name, invoice number, part number, current balance, etc.). The report program then sorts the file by these items into a temporary file. The report is always generated from this file using the same layout, but the sequence of the data reported varies, depending on the sort field selected. In this manner, one program can generate many different reports.

The following four reports should be present as a minimum:

(1) Aged receivables sorted by customer. There should be one detail line for each customer showing the amount of receivables due in each of several time periods. The first period should be from 0 to 30 days. More complete reports will divide this category into two: 0 to 10 days and 10 to 30 days. The succeeding time slots should be 30 to 60 days, 60 to 90 days, 90 to 120 days, 120 to 180 days, and over 180 days. The total for each time slot should appear at the bottom. A nice additional feature on this report is a line below the totals showing percent of total receivables in this category and a final average number of days in receivables.

This report will show you at a glance who is late in paying and by how much. Another convenient feature on an aged accounts receivable report is the inclusion of each outstanding invoice for a customer above the customer's summary line, preferably sorted by date. This shows at a glance which invoices are overdue for a given customer; a useful report for your collections department.

(2) Current customer status report. This report should show all of the information in the customer master file, as well as the total dollar amount of outstanding receivables from the invoice master file.

(3) Invoice printing. Believe it or not, many systems will not print your invoices for you. This means entering the data twice: once on the invoice form in the typewriter and once on the CRT for entry into the file. An additional complication is that you either have to get preprinted invoices in the format that the invoice printing program prints them (change your business to fit the program) or else have the program modified to fit your own forms (pay someone to change the program to fit your business). Either way, the savings in clerical time and increased accuracy make this feature mandatory. (The computer will edit many of the inputs to the receivables system, remember?)

(4) Audit report. The value and purpose of audit trails were discussed earlier. There is no system in which complete audit reports are more important than accounts receivable. Think very carefully about buying a system that does not offer them.

The presence of the optional fields on the various accounts receivable files allows the generation of many other useful reports:

(1) Gross margin by part number. This can be derived from the invoice detail file, using the unit-price and unit-cost fields. It should be

sortable at your option in part number, descending gross margin, or quantity sold sequence.

(2) Sales analysis. From the month-to-date and year-to-date fields in the customer master, a report can be generated showing to whom you have sold the most goods or services. In addition, using the cost-of-sales field to generate gross margin figures shows you who your most profitable customers are (not necessarily the same).

(3) Credit report. From credit limit, high balance, average days outstanding receivables, and date of last payment, a useful report can be generated.

(4) Shipper printing. Again there is the same problem with preprinted or customized forms. There is also the inconvenience of changing back and forth from shippers to invoices. However, the advantages are the same as for printing invoices: accuracy and reduction of clerical work.

(5) Mailing labels. This is such a simple program to write that I think every seller of accounts receivable software should include it gratis. It should print the customer names and addresses on standard-sized (3½″ x 15/16″), one-across, pressure-sensitive labels. Having this feature leads to all sorts of creative marketing ideas. It should also be available to the accounts payable vendor master file, another file containing names and addresses.

All printed reports that present a volume of summary information for an entire file should be available as a retrieval to the CRT on a selective basis. That is, the aged accounts receivable report should be called to the screen by individual customer, as should the information in the customer master file.

Additional reports from the receivables system are limited only by your imagination and willingness either to learn to program them yourself (not as hard as you might think, using the existing programs as models for variations of already existing reports) or to pay someone to do it for you. However, remember that you cannot report information that is not in the system. This means that the files designed into your system and the data items present in the files put the upper limit on what can be done with your system. This makes the record layouts the most important element of the system, and deserving of the greatest proportion of your analysis time.

Processes. Most of the programs in your accounts receivable system are defined by the input and output requirements. Obviously, one program is required for each report and screen retrieval. In addition, one file maintenance program (a program that performs the four functions: add, change, delete, and display) is required for every file. Finally, one program is required for each input function: a program to enter invoices, a program to enter cash receipts, etc.

Also required are end-of-period processing programs, such as the end-of-month routine. This program should, for example, add all month-to-date information to the quarter-to-date and year-to-date fields, and zero the month-to-date fields. The procedures for running these programs should be clear and as nearly foolproof as possible. They generally produce irreversible changes to your files. Another example of this type of program posts your receivables information to the general ledger. While evaluating a particular package, try running these programs twice in a row to see how difficult the writers of the system have made it for you to mess up the procedure.

Inputs. Inputs cause the most immediate change in the way you do business when you use a computer system. Most of the manual support system to be designed around the automated system involves the means of getting the source documents to the computer and entering them on time. To accomplish this you will have to analyze your paper flow and change it to be routed by the computer. Personnel will have to be trained to input the data. It almost always results in an increased load on the staff, at least initially, because two systems (the old one and the new one) have to be maintained. Hopefully, after the system is completely implemented, some of the drudge work that has been using up your employees' time will be taken over by the computer.

In the case of accounts receivable, the primary source document will be a sales order to be invoiced. When testing a prospective system, use your own sales orders to see if all the information required by the program is present on your form.

You will also need to enter payments, credits, and adjustments. This means another change in procedure. As part of the processing of cash receipts from customers you must now enter this information into the computer. The procedure must ensure that this is done for each receipt and that it will not be done twice. The program should give you some indication that you are making an overpayment, but don't rely on the program to ensure proper operation of your system. If there is some way to defeat a system, people will generally find it in the first 2 days of operation.

ORDER ENTRY SYSTEM

An order entry system is really a front-end extension to your accounts receivable system, since the order is generally booked and entered into the data files before an invoice is printed. As such, it should have several points of interface with the accounts receivable data. This implies that both sets of files should be on-line at the same time. Some systems will not allow you to enter an invoice before the sales order is entered. Other systems do not have this requirement. Some users prefer the former method and some the latter. Whichever you prefer, test the system for this feature to make sure you can live with the way it is designed. The principle advantages of an order entry system are the automated printing of sales orders and the sales history reporting.

Storage. Two files are required: the sales order master file and the sales order detail file. (See Figures 35 and 36.) Implied is the presence of a bill-to and perhaps a ship-to-name-and-address file from the accounts receivable system. Almost never will you find a sales order entry system offered without an accounts receivable package.

The key to the order entry master file is the sales order number. Some systems will automatically assign this number in sequence by keeping track of the last number assigned. This will prevent duplicate use of numbers and eliminate the need to assign blocks of numbers to different areas of the business where sales orders might be generated. As noted before, this file should link to the bill-to-name-and-address file, as well as to the ship-to-name-and-address file and the invoice master in accounts receivable. The invoice number should be inserted in this field at the time the invoice is entered into the accounts receivable system. The customer's purchase order number, the freight and tax amounts, and the special instruction lines must be filled in so they can be printed on your preprinted sales order forms.

The entry date can become useful historical information. Coupled with the invoice date, it can produce a report showing the lead time between receipt of a sales order and the ship date (assuming you invoice on the same day you ship, and if not, why not?). Coupled with the promised ship date, it becomes a quick, real-time argument settler with customers who ask where their orders are.

The hold flag can indicate a number of things, depending on its value. Among them are: (1) This sales order is in the rough state and may be subject to revisions, (2) Don't release this sale pending credit approval, (3) This order is okay to fill and ship, (4) This order has been shipped and invoiced, etc. If properly programmed, this field can be a very useful monitoring tool for your sales order function.

The sales order detail file contains one record for each line item on the sales order. By concatenating the sales order number and the line item, you produce a unique key that can be used to retrieve this line item later. The part number should be present but may or may not link to an on-line item master file containing the description. If not, the part's description should also be present in the detail file.

OPT	KEY	LINK	DESCRIPTION
	*		Sales order number
		*	Bill-to-customer number
			Order date
			Customer purchase order number
			Freight amount
			Tax amount
			Special instructions line 1
			Special instructions line 2
			Special instructions line 3
*		*	Ship-to-customer number
*			Entry date
*			Promised ship date
*			Hold flag
*			FOB
*			Ship via
*			Invoice number
*			Sales agent
*			Commission amount

Figure 35. Sales order master file.

The purposes of the unit price and quantity are self-explanatory. The program should calculate the extensions from the line item and the quantity. The presence of these data in the record would waste space and is an indicator of poor design. If unit cost is present in the accounts receivable system, it is probably redundant. Quantity shipped is an important feature, as it allows you to produce backlog reports. If backlog is an important item in your business, be sure the system has some way of tracking quantity shipped.

The special-instructions fields on both files will vary in length and number from system to system. By bringing in some of your live sales orders and entering them while evaluating a system, you'll readily see if the length and number of fields are adequate.

An additional file not shown in the layouts is the sales-agent file. If present, the sales-agent field in the order entry master record becomes a link to the sales-agent file, which contains information such as name and address (handy if you have a large organization of sales representatives), territory, and perhaps a commission schedule.

Outputs.
(1) The most important output is the printing of the sales order. If the system does not do this, why buy it?

OPT	KEY	LINK	DESCRIPTION
{ *	*		Sales order number
{ *			Line item
		*	Part number
			Quantity ordered
			Unit price
			Special instructions line 1
			Special instructions line 2
*			Description
*			Unit cost
*			Quantity shipped

Figure 36.   Sales order detail file.

(2) The next most important is a screen retrieval of a sales order and its status. This is the kind of instant answer that makes a small business system so valuable.

(3) Sales history reporting. Since it's going to take a considerable effort (meaning dollars) to enter all these data into your system, it would be a shame not to have some way to analyze them when they reach a significant volume. You will want to see who is buying what and how much of it, and which product lines are the most and least profitable (this requires access to unit-cost information if it is not in the detail file).

(4) Commissions reporting. Who is selling the most, what are they selling the most of, and how much are they earning in commissions?

(5) Backlog reporting. This should be sortable by any combination of customer, part number, and promised ship date.

Process. Besides the usual data-entry programs, report-generating programs, and the add, change, delete, and display from the name-and-address files, other features you might want to look for are:

(1) Overlay of commissions to the accounts payable and/or general ledger programs.

(2) Overlay of booked and/or shipped sales to the general ledger.

(3) Edit checking to ensure valid part numbers, customer number, sales-agent (if there is a sales agent) file, and dates.

Also, the programs should do a preliminary credit check and warn the operator if there is a problem.

Inputs. The primary input here is some sort of sales order rough. If you don't have a standard sales order rough form on which you hand-write the customer's order as it comes in by phone or mail, you might want to design one. It should follow the layout of the screen display that prompts for the input of a sales order. This would make the entry easier and faster for the data entry clerk, as well as ensure that whoever is making out the sales order does it in a consistent manner. (Sometimes several different people will enter data, even in a small organization.) Again, as with receivables, this document must be routed at some point past the data entry clerk at the computer.

Finally, quantity shipped must be updated as shipments go out. This means routing a copy of the shipper to the data entry clerk.

At this point, the importance of your manual procedures should be obvious. As you gain confidence in your computer and its data, you will automatically be assuming that it's telling you the truth. If a shipper does not get entered, that sales order will always appear in the data files as being unshipped. It may never get invoiced. For this reason, give at least as much thought and effort to the design and implementation of your manual support procedures as to the selection of hardware and software when automating.

ACCOUNTS PAYABLE SYSTEM

A well-written accounts payable system can provide major benefits to your business. Two of the most common small business problems are controlling cash flow (particularly expenditures) and the tracking and taking of discounts from vendors. The discount amounts are sometimes so small that the manual effort required to keep track of them exceeds the amount of the discount. However, taken in the aggregate, they can amount to some very significant figures. On the cash disbursements side, payments that are either too tightly controlled ("I think I'll just stretch these folks out a little more") or under-controlled ("I wonder what I did with that stack of unpaids from last month?") can cause not only loss of discounts, but loss of credit rating and sometimes loss of important vendors. A final problem in this area concerns the projection of cash requirements. This is one painstaking task in which the computer can be of material benefit.

Storage. The accounts payable master file layout (see Figure 37) shows three items as key fields. The best way to access this file is by invoice number. However, purchase order and voucher number run a close second and third. The ideal system allows for multiple keys, such that information can be retrieved from this file by specifying any one of the three key fields. Multiple keys for random access files is a feature not yet seen on many micro-based systems, although there is no reason why it

OPT	KEY	LINK	DESCRIPTION
	*		Invoice number
*	*		Voucher number
*	*	*	Purchase order number
		*	Vendor number
			Invoice amount
			Discount dollars
			Discount due date
			Take discount (Y/N)
			Payment due date
*			Invoice date
*		*	Vendor remit number
*			Hold flag
*			Check date
*			Check number
*			G/L account number
*			G/L amount

Figure 37. Accounts payable master file.

can't be implemented. Ask your computer dealer about this feature. If he or she doesn't know what you're talking about, find another dealer.

In addition to being an optional key field, the purchase order number also serves as a link to the purchase order system, if you have one. Likewise, the vendor number links to a vendor-name-and-address file, eliminating the need to have the vendor's name and address appear in each record with the resultant waste of space. A file layout showing the vendor's name and address in the master record is a sign of poor design.

The invoice amount and discount dollars are self-explanatory. I consider the two fields, discount due date and payment due date, to be absolutely essential. Without them the system cannot solve the basic problem of who gets paid when. The addition of a "take discount" flag provides some conveniences that can be partially compensated for by programming. One value of this flag indicates that you are to take the discount, another value indicates that you are not. This is useful in generating reports showing who is to be paid. Without it, you generally either specify that all discounts are to be taken/not taken or you select which are to be paid on an invoice-by-invoice basis.

The hold flag is a fairly common feature. It allows you to put a vendor's invoice on hold indefinitely. It either will not appear on your "to be paid" report or will appear as overdue but on hold. The check date and check number should be entered into the record by the program at the time the check is cut.

The vendor remit number points to the vendor's record in the vendor

OPT	KEY	LINK	DESCRIPTION
	*		Remit-to-vendor number
*		*	Vendor number
			Remit-to-name
			Remit-to-address line 1
			Remit-to-address line 2
*			Remit-to-address line 3
			Remit-to-city, state
			Remit-to-zip

Figure 38.   Remit to name and address file.

remit-to file. (See Figure 38.) If there is no purchasing system available, this file will probably look more like the vendor master file from the purchasing system. With a purchasing system present, the vendor number field provides a cross-link to the purchasing vendor file.

The check file (see Figure 39) is essential not only as a record of who has been paid what, but also for your bank account reconciliation.

Outputs.
(1) Check printing is the most obvious function of your payables system. If you don't cut many checks, however, you may want to continue to write them by hand from a report showing who is to be paid. Otherwise you have the same problem as in the receivables and order entry systems of either purchasing the forms to fit the check printing program or changing the program to fit your checks.

In either case, a comprehensive post-check writing report should be produced as an audit trail to show which check numbers were produced, to whom they were written, the amounts of the checks, the dates they were cut, the invoice numbers, and perhaps the purchase order numbers.

(2) Accounts payable status report. This report should show the status of each record in the accounts-payable master file. There are several ways to sort it to produce a useful report. One way is to group all the unpaid items together, followed by all the paid items. Another way is by invoice number or voucher number sequence. One of the best ways is by due date. This will show at a glance who is overdue for their money and who will soon be due. This report should be formatted to make it easy for you to see which invoices to pay to get the discount, which are on hold, and which are overdue. It should display the invoice and discount amounts, as well as any partial payments against the invoice. An accounts payable aging report in a format similar to the aged accounts receivable report provides a fast look at your future cash requirements.

OPT	KEY	LINK	DESCRIPTION
	*		Check number
		*	Invoice number
			Check date
			Amount
			Status

Figure 39. Check file.

(3) Pre-check writing report. This report should be generated before printing checks. It shows you, given your payment criteria, the checks that will be printed by the next run of the check-writing program, and it gives you a chance to override or add to the list.

(4) Vendor name-and-address list. This is self-explanatory. Your system should provide an option for printing the names and addresses on standard-sized labels.

Process. The procedures established by the design of the program are more critical than in most other systems since they involve cash disbursements. While evaluating a system, pay particularly close attention to what safeguards exist to prevent double payment and entry and payment of fraudulent invoices. This is most effectively accomplished through the use of passwords. One password required to execute any program in the system may be sufficient to prevent fraud. Passwords on individual programs provide a greater level of security by allowing only certain persons to enter invoices, while allowing others to print the checks or update the vendor master file. Passwords should be easily and conveniently changeable by the user.

The system should have a facility built in to allow the processing of hand-written checks. In the real world, no matter how efficient or automated your payables are, you will always have occasion to write checks by hand. In that event, a program should exist to allow the entry and processing of this type of transaction, without having to go through some awkward gyration to accommodate the standard procedure.

A very desirable feature is the check reconciliation program, which accounts for returned, cancelled, void, and outstanding checks. This can be a real time-saver, particularly from the accuracy standpoint.

There is generally some kind of end-of-period processing that gathers and transmits data to the general ledger and zeros out month-to-date and year-to-date fields. The procedures for this function should be carefully followed. Its effects are generally not easily reversible. This implies, of course, that the best systems are those that provide safeguards against human error.

There should be a program to determine which vouchers are to be paid based on some parameters that are under your control. Most common is the date window, a start date, and an end date, within which all due or overdue invoices are selected for payment.

The system should include, as a minimum, one CRT retrieval program (a program that retrieves data from a file and displays it on the CRT) to display the status of any vendor's account and, of course, the ability to add, change, and delete vendor master records.

Inputs. Again, the critical nature of the payables system demands rigorous edit checking, not only for valid vendor and general ledger account numbers, but also for reasonableness of figures. A truly sophisticated system will check the amount to be paid against the purchase order and the standard cost in the inventory file and display a warning if the variance is too great.

Controlling the input source documents is a relatively easy task, since there is only one — the vendor's invoice. Whoever is responsible for matching the invoice with the purchase order and verifying that the goods or services have been received should probably also be responsible for the input and generation of the checks for the controller's signature.

PURCHASING SYSTEM

Purchasing-system software for microprocessor-based systems is currently pretty scarce. It is difficult to write and up until now the market has been small. As the power of the hardware increases and the prices decrease, more and more businesses will be using micro-based systems. The number of transactions required to make this application cost-effective will become smaller and smaller. Businesses that will be writing enough purchase orders and businesses in which the timely delivery of purchased material is essential will find an automated purchasing system to be a real asset.

The purchasing system performs two major functions. First, it organizes and edits the entry of a purchase order — checking for valid part numbers, reasonable costs, and correct dates. It also performs the arithmetic and prints out neat, legible purchase orders on your preprinted, continuous forms. Second, through the reporting features, it allows you to monitor the status of your purchase orders, notifying you when shipments are overdue.

Like the complementary accounts receivable and sales order systems, several points of interface between the purchasing and accounts payable system are desirable. This implies again that both systems are on-line and may require the storage capacity of a hard disk, with a capacity in the megabyte range.

OPT	KEY	LINK	DESCRIPTION
	*		Purchase order number
*			Hold flag
		*	Vendor number
			Open/closed flag
*			Date of order
*		*	Remit-to vendor number
*			Buyer code

Figure 40.   Purchase order master file.

Storage.   Here again you can see the advantages of the master/detail file scheme. (See Figures 40 and 41.) The purchase order master file uses the purchase order number as the primary key, since all purchase orders are uniquely identified by this number. The hold flag allows the entry of purchase orders in rough form and prevents them from being printed until all the information required has been assembled. The vendor number provides a link to the vendor file, thus eliminating the space-wasting inclusion of the vendor's name and address in each master record.

The open/closed flag is an easy way to indicate whether all items on this purchase order have been received, or, if not, that no further deliveries on this purchase order are desired.

If the date of order is not included, it should at least show on the audit report of purchase orders entered. The remit-to vendor number is used by the accounts payable system. When paying a vendor's invoice, it will access the purchase order master file at the time you enter the purchase order number to be paid. It can then pick up the remit-to-name-and-address for printing on the check or stub.

The buyer code is generally the buyer's initials and provides a quick way to see who is responsible for ordering this material and tracking its delivery.

OPT	KEY	LINK	DESCRIPTION
	{ *	*	Purchase order number
	{ *		Line item number
			Unit price
			Quantity ordered
			Vendor promised date
			Quantity received
*			Quantity returned to vendor
*			Date of last receipt
*			Job number

Figure 41.   Purchase order detail file.

In the purchase order detail file we find one record for every line item on a purchase order. Concatenating the purchase order number with the line item number produces a unique key for retrieving information from this file. The unit price and quantity are self-explanatory. The vendor-promised delivery date is essential to create a report of purchase orders by due date — one of the primary advantages of an automated purchase order system. The quantity received should be updated each time goods are received against this purchase order. The quantity returned to vendor is not only desirable for screen retrievals to check the status of a purchase order, but can also be used to generate a report that evaluates a vendor's performance over time. The date of last receipt is useful if you open blanket purchase orders covering multiple deliveries over long periods of time.

If your business is one that tracks costs by job, such as a construction contractor, then the inclusion of the job-number field allows you to assign material costs to a particular job and report it later. Couple this with a mechanism to track labor costs, such as a labor-distribution program, and you have the basic elements present to implement a complete job-cost tracking system.

We've seen enough name and address files by now to recognize most of the fields in the vendor master file. (See Figure 42.) Note that there are several fields that are more properly utilized by the accounts payable system, which I have assumed to be on-line with the purchase orders; namely, the discount percentage, discount days, and net days. For systems with no purchasing software, you should expect to see this information in the accounts payable files. The month-to-date and year-to-date payments accumulate data for historical reports and analyses of your vendors.

Outputs. Of course the most utilitarian function that this purchase order system can perform for you is to print your purchase orders on your preprinted forms in a neat, correct, and legible manner. Again, this presents the conflict of whether to use the program's standard purchase order form or to rewrite the purchase order printing program to suit your own forms.

The next most important item is a purchase order status report sorted by due date. If you have multiple buyers, the primary sort key should be by buyer code and the secondary key by due date. You can then run this report each day or week, tear it apart by buyer code, and give each buyer a list showing which purchase orders are overdue, which are due today or this week, and which are not due for a while. This is also a useful report for anyone in the company who is waiting on the delivery of parts to continue or complete some task, like an assembly or the shipment of a sales order.

There are several other useful flavors of this report. A sort by part

OPT	KEY	LINK	DESCRIPTION
	*		Vendor number
			Vendor name
			Vendor address line 1
			Vendor address line 2
*			Vendor address line 3
			Vendor city, state
			Vendor zip
*			Telephone number
*			Discount percentage
*			Discount days
*			Net days
*		*	Remit-to vendor number
*			Month-to-date payments
*			Month-to-date discounts
*			Year-to-date payments
*			Year-to-date discounts

Figure 42. Vendor name and address file.

number will show all the open purchase orders for a given part. It will give you an idea of how much of a part is on order, whether too many vendors are being used, or the quantities ordered are too small. In companies that cut a lot of purchase orders, this report can result in considerable savings.

Process. In addition to the standard add, change, delete, and display program for the vendor master file, programs are required to enter, edit, and print the purchase orders. The receiving program should check the item received against the purchase order to see that the item was indeed ordered. Overshipments should be rejected by the program.

Inputs. The principal input to the system is the purchase order. If a purchase requisition form is used, it will greatly facilitate the entry of the purchase order. Otherwise, it is important to have some sort of source document from which to key in the purchase order. The actual entry will probably be done by a clerk rather than a buyer, and as such, the possibilities for errors from an unclear source document are great.

The other item to be input is a dock receipt, packing slip, or other document showing the receipt of an item on a purchase order. Here again, manual procedures that ensure the entry of *every* receipt are critical. In general, an accounts payable system should not pay for items that are indicated as unreceived in the purchase order detail file.

INVENTORY SYSTEM

This is one of the simplest yet most useful systems. It requires, of course, that you have enough inventory items and enough movement in them to have problems with stock-outs, incorrect quantities on hand, shrinkage, etc., to justify the expense and effort required to automate your inventory.

Storage. Only one file is required — the item master. (See Figure 43.) Each item in your inventory will have one record in the item master file. In its simplest form the record contains only three fields: the part number (used as the key to retrieve inventory information), the description, and the quantity on hand.

Some of the optional fields that enhance the usefulness of the system are the primary and secondary sources for this part (in the form of the vendor number, which links to the vendor master file). These are particularly valuable if the purchasing system is on-line. The standard material and labor costs (if any) provide the cornerstone of a standard cost accounting system. The order point/safety stock should trigger a request to order when quantity on hand is equal to or less than this figure, and the quantity on order is, again, particularly useful if the purchasing system is present. The function of the ABC and cycle-count fields are described below in the section on cycle counting.

The total usage month-to-date and year-to-date keeps a running total of the quantity of an item issued from stock. These figures can be used to assemble sales data in the absence of sales order history reporting and inventory usage reports.

Outputs. The most useful output of the inventory system is a screen retrieval showing the current quantity on hand (and quantity on order, if available). It should also show the invariant information, such as reorder point and unit cost.

Another useful report is the order action report, which lists all items in inventory that have reached the order point or safety stock level. These should be calculated based on inventory usage figures and purchasing lead times.

If usage figures are present, the system should provide comprehensive inventory usage reports. The most useful form of this report sorts the output in descending dollar value of inventory used, which places those items that account for the greatest dollar value of your inventory at the top of the report.

Recognizing that most businesses take a physical inventory at least once a year, thoughtful inventory system designers include a physical inventory report. This contains the item number and description and the

OPT	KEY	LINK	DESCRIPTION
	*		Part number
			Description
			Quantity on hand
*			Cycle count date
*			ABC code
*			Primary vendor
*			Second source
*			Material cost
*			Labor cost
*			Order point/safety stock
*			Quantity on order
*			Total usage month-to-date
*			Total usage year-to-date

Figure 43. Inventory item master file.

quantity on hand in the file. It provides a space to write in the quantity actually counted, the counter's initials, and the date of counting.

Process. The programs required to operate this system are as simple as the file itself: one program to add, change, delete, and display item master records; one program for the receipt and issue of items from stock; and several report programs. Audit trails are of paramount importance in this system. There is no way for the system to edit the quantities issued from or received to stock, other than not allowing the quantity on hand to drop below zero and placing a maximum on the quantity so issued or received (to prevent the receipt of 100,000 when 1,000 was really intended). Since errors in input are inevitable, you'll want to have an orderly way to trace back all of the transactions against this file.

Inputs. The inputs to the system come from two sources: the issues from inventory and receipts to inventory. Since these two activities are generally physically separated — one being at the receiving dock and the other at the stores window or perhaps at the sales counter — a lot of thought should be given to establishing a manual system that will cause all inventory movement to be entered into your inventory files.

Since you may have very little luck getting people to stop whatever they are doing, walk to the computer, and input their transactions each time they move an inventory item, some sort of source documents are in order. These can be routed to the data entry clerk's in-basket by the terminal. For receipts, this can be the shipping documents or dock receipts, or perhaps a receiving log that is kept at the dock. For issues, the sales order filled out by the sales person can serve as a source document. Legibility is the biggest problem here.

Unfortunately, these procedures put you into a batch processing mode, which means that you input all the transactions for a half or a whole day at one time. This in turn means losing the benefits of an on-line system, but it solves the input problem. It is preferable to have purchasing, inventory, and sales order systems on-line (implying a hard disk with multi-megabyte capacity), so that inventory levels are automatically increased by receipts against purchase orders and decreased by issuance of sales orders. A hardware solution is to purchase a system that supports several terminals. Then you can place one terminal by receiving and one at the sales counter or shipping dock, where it can be conveniently accessed by those who need it.

CYCLE COUNTING

Cycle counting is an extremely efficient method of getting a handle on your inventories when the number of items is very large and more than one physical inventory per year is impractical. It amounts to a sort of perpetual physical inventory, where the computer directs that certain items in inventory be counted every day.

Cycle counting is based on the 80/20 rule that is so common to many facets of business. This rule states that 80% of something relates to 20% of something else. For example, 80% of your sales come from 20% of your customers. You make 80% of your purchases come from 20% of your suppliers; 80% of the foul-ups in your business can be traced to 20% of the employees in your 5-person staff. In your inventory, 80% of the total dollars of inventory value can be accounted for by only 20% of the items. Therefore, if you were to monitor only one-fifth of the items in your inventory, the ones that account for four-fifths of your inventory dollars, you would have control over 80% of the inventory costs.

The first step in implementing a cycle counting system for your inventory is to divide your items into three categories: A, B, and C. The 'A' items will account for 80% of your inventory dollars and will comprise about 20% of the items. The 'B' items will account for the next 15% of inventory value and may include another 30%. The 'C' items include all the rest. There are two ways to determine inventory value: quantity-on-hand times unit-cost, and inventory usage over time. The first method can be implemented immediately; the second requires historical data that can be accumulated by your system if you don't already have it.

These 80%, 15%, 5% divisions are not hard and fast figures and should be adjusted to provide you with the most useful data. The next decision is how often to count the three categories. A good rule of thumb is to count the 'A' items four times a year, the 'B' items twice a year, and the 'C' items once a year. Again, these frequencies should be adjusted to meet your particular needs and the programs should accommodate these adjustments.

After assigning the 'ABC' code and determining the frequency of counting for the three classes, it is necessary to initialize the cycle count date for each item. This is done by taking all of the items in a given class and spreading their dates of last cycle count evenly over the last time period of their count. For example, if today's date is July 1, 1980, and it has been decided that the 'A' items will be counted four times a year, then the date that the first 'A' item was last cycle counted would be set to April 1, three months earlier. April 2 should be assigned to the next 'A' item, April 3 to the next, and so on, until July 1 is reached. The next 'A' item in the list would get the date April 1, and so on. The same procedure would be followed for the 'B' items, starting with January 1, 1980, and for the 'C' items, starting with July 1, 1979. At the end of this procedure, the dates of last cycle count will be spread evenly over all of the inventory items.

The above tasks should be accomplished programmatically. The inventory valuation report will show the division of the inventory by dollar value. Another program should assign the 'ABC' codes based on your criteria for the categories. Another program should spread the cycle count dates over time.

Each day, a final program should scan the entire inventory file and check, based on today's date and the date of last cycle count, which items are due for counting. Since the cycle count date initiator spreads the date of last cycle count dates over the entire preceding period for that group, several of the items will come out on the first day and several more each succeeding day.

The final program to complete the loop accepts the results of the physical count, updates the quantity on hand to match what was physically counted, and produces a report showing the quantity and dollar amount at standard cost by which your inventory was increased or decreased. Finally, the program inserts today's date as the date of last cycle count. This item will then come up again for counting in 3, 6, or 12 months, depending on its 'ABC' code.

I have not yet seen this particular method implemented on a microprocessor system, I suppose partly because the software industry has not yet realized that they have small machines powerful enough to handle businesses requiring such inventory control techniques. However, if you understand the process, it should not be too difficult to design the system and contract it out to be programmed. You would then have a very marketable product with which to recover your costs of development (and then some, perhaps).

THE GENERAL LEDGER

The general ledger forms the backbone of the accounting system. However, automating it in your environment may or may not produce enough of a payoff to warrant the effort required to implement it. Remember, systems such as receivables and payables are really subledgers. The final figures from these systems are usually posted to the general ledger on a monthly basis. These figures — along with the inventory balances, cash on hand (bank statement), and accumulated depreciation from your fixed asset tracking system — are available in, and must be gathered from, other sources. The general ledger produces summary figures which, if there are any questions, must be broken down from their corresponding subledgers or journal entries. If your financial statements are taking only a few hours each month to assemble, you may want to forego the general ledger altogether. Extensive testing of various packages is the only way to determine if the effort is worth it for you.

Storage. In principle, this is a very simple system, requiring only two files — a general ledger account master file and a general ledger posting detail file. (See Figures 44 and 45.)

In its most primitive form, the general ledger account master contains only three fields — the general ledger number, which should act as a key field, the description to be printed on the financial statements, and the year-to-date balance. The month-to-date balance I consider essential information to make the general ledger reports worth the effort of putting in the data.

Two features can extend the capabilities of your general ledger to provide useful outputs. The field called "this year's actuals by month" is actually 12 separate fields, although I don't show that on the file layout. They are used to collect each month's actual figures for reporting later on, particularly in comparison to the budgeted figures.

The 12 months of budget figures provide a facility to do something that almost all businesses need and most forgo due to the time and effort involved — long-range planning. Establishing goals to work toward and guidelines to follow, and then tracking these projections against the actual results give two positive benefits.

First, this forces you to sit down and project the state of your business 1 year into the future. What should sales be in 1 year? How will that affect headcount and consequently the payroll? How much working capital will be required to fund increases in inventory? What capital investments need to be made? Given these assumptions, how profitable is the business? Is this really better than a McDonald's franchise or retiring to Key West with a fistful of Treasury bills?

OPT	KEY	LINK	DESCRIPTION
	*	*	Account number
			Account description
			Month-to-date actual
			Year-to-date actual
*			This year's actuals by month
*			Twelve months budget figures
*			Normal balance (credit/debit)

Figure 44. General ledger account master file.

Second, as the year progresses, tracking actuals against plans will give you fast feedback on where your business is going off the track. Is there some good reason why payroll is 30% above plan? Receivables are 25% under budget, but so are sales. Is the credit policy too tight?

Not shown on the master file layout, but generally present in one form or another, is some field that helps the programs decide where this account goes on a particular report and/or whether this is a detail, subtotal, or total line.

The programming problem to be solved in this system is how to create financial reports while still allowing the users to define their own general ledger account numbering system. Some program designs simplify this problem by locking you into one form of general ledger account number format, the contents of which have some intelligence (i.e., all balance sheet accounts start with 1, all revenue accounts with 2, all expense accounts with 3, etc.). The program then interprets this number as a guide to formatting the reports.

Check carefully the design constraints built into the account numbering scheme to determine if you can change your system to fit the computer's.

The other file, the ubiquitous detail file, which seems to follow every master file around like a puppy dog, has only three essential fields — the general ledger account number (the key field that links back to the general

OPT	KEY	LINK	DESCRIPTION
	*	*	G/L account number
*	*		Transaction number
*			Posting reference
			Fiscal month and year
*			Credit/debit flag
			Posting amount

Figure 45. General ledger posting detail file.

ledger master file), the fiscal month and year to which this transaction belongs, and the posting amount. Some systems use some kind of transaction, voucher, or folio number as a key to keep the postings straight and as an additional key. Some systems also use a credit/debit flag as one way of solving the biggest programming headache in the whole business software industry — when to add and when to subtract amounts from general ledger account balances.

Outputs. The financial statements are the obvious outputs — balance sheets and income statements, at a minimum. They should show month-to-date and year-to-date. Also useful on these reports is "this month versus last month" and "budget versus actual."

I would be very cautious about a general ledger system that did not also produce a trial balance. This report should be run at the end of an accounting period and should show each account in the file, along with all of the transactions posted against that count for the period.

Detail postings by account will give you auditability on how you got from one month's figures to the next, but a complete transaction audit report is a must for a general ledger system.

If the 12 months of budget and actual are included in the files, you should also have monthly spread reports comparing budget to actual. The financial statements should also show these budgeted amounts to compare to actuals.

Process. The sequence of events in operating your general ledger can be tricky because the detail postings accumulated all month must be added to (or subtracted from) last month's account balances, and the end-of-month figures are generally rolled into a year-to-date. Sometimes a rolling 12 months of data is kept on file. This means that backing up in case of a mistake can be difficult or impossible. This is one system that it pays to try before you buy. I have seen some that were so confusing in their operation that it was almost impossible to do it right. The problems generally occur when month-to-date fields are set to zero. If it is left to your discretion to zero them after rolling them into year-to-date, I guarantee you'll double post them at least once a year.

Many systems will use a batch approach, storing each transaction as it is keyed in and giving the operator a total debits and credits figure at the end of a batch of transactions for verification. If the total is OK, the system will then go ahead and post all the transactions at one time. There is a lot to be said for this approach in this particular system. Under no circumstances should the system allow you to post transactions that are out of balance.

Inputs. The sources of input to the general ledger are many and varied. Generally, this system is best operated by the bookkeeper, an accountant, or even the controller or treasurer. It should be simple and straightforward enough to allow even highly educated people to use it.

It should also be programmed to interface directly with the accounts receivable, accounts payable, and payroll systems, which should have some command to prepare summary records to be transmitted to the detail posting file. A high degree of systems integration is very desirable here.

The toughest part of implementing a general ledger will probably be the input of the general ledger account master. Usually the conventions required by the writers of the system to identify the type of account, its level of indenting on the reports, and its normal balance, seem a little awkward. You will probably want to lay out your financial statements first and assign account numbers to them before implementing this system. A well-documented system will have a well-written, step-by-step process for you to follow and worksheets to help organize your initial input.

PAYROLL

There is nothing that makes employees unhappier than to have their paychecks fouled up, unless it's having them fouled up by a computer. Of all the packages discussed so far, payroll is probably the trickiest to write, to set up, and to run. Ten rounds with a form 1040 will tell you why. Anything the government does . . . well, never mind. Weigh very carefully the advantages and benefits to be gained by automating this function. Having an outside service do your payroll may even be preferable to bringing it in-house in some cases. A glance at the file layout will show you why.

Storage. The payroll master file shown here (see Figure 46) is by no means the last word in payroll files. In fact, I have tried to simplify it as much as possible. The number of required fields gives rise to many possibilities for error on input.

The file can be considered in two sections: (1) the employee information that remains constant (or relatively so) from pay period to pay period, and (2) the various month-to-date, quarter-to-date, and year-to-date fields, which accumulate the totals paid to and deducted from the employees.

The employee numbers, if your company is big enough to have them, will generally serve as the key to the payroll master, although the idea of using social security numbers as employee numbers is gaining in pop-

OPT	KEY	LINK	DESCRIPTION
	*		Employee number or social security number
			Name
			Address
			City
			State
			Federal exemptions
			State exemptions
			Pay rate
			Hourly/weekly/bi-weekly
			Deduction 1
			Deduction 2
*			Date hired
*			Date terminated
*			Sex
*			Marital status
*			Ethnic code
*			Position code
			MTD/QTD/YTD straight earnings
			MTD/QTD/YTD overtime earnings
			MTD/QTD/YTD other earnings
			MTD/QTD/YTD miscellaneous income
			MTD/QTD/YTD FICA deductions
			MTD/QTD/YTD federal withholding
			MTD/QTD/YTD state withholding
			MTD/QTD/YTD city withholding
			MTD/QTD/YTD deduction 1
			MTD/QTD/YTD deduction 2

Figure 46. Payroll master file.

ularity. After all, *someone* spent a lot of our money setting up a system to give everyone a unique number. Why not use it?

The name and address are standard and essential. I have shown two exemptions; state and federal. The pay rate is of course required, as is some sort of code to tell whether this rate is hourly, weekly, biweekly, semiweekly, etc. A multiplicity of deduction fields are represented by two general ones. Check the capabilities of any system you evaluate for the maximum number and type of deductions allowed.

Much of the optional material in this file relates to equal employment opportunity information. Having this information on file, along with the required reports, can save your company a lot of time and money.

The month-to-date, quarter-to-date, and year-to-date fields are by no means as all-inclusive as shown. I have included two of the most common ones to give you an idea of what should be present. This is one system where being able to see and understand the record layouts will give you the quickest overview of the system's capabilities.

I did not even attempt to lay out the payroll tax tables (see Figure 47). There are many, many different schemes for doing this. Suffice it to say that these tables must be present. It is vitally important that the vendor of a payroll package provide a continuous update service for these tables, as tax rates almost certainly vary from year to year.

This means that a well-established, stable software outfit with a payroll package that has been in the field for several years will have the inside track in your selection process. You will want to be sure not only that the package works correctly, but that 5 years from now you will still be getting your tax table updates from them. The best way to check out this aspect of a payroll system is by reference. Find 3 or 4 people who are running this payroll package and watch it operate on-site. It will be very instructive.

Outputs. The most important output of this system is, of course, the paychecks. Here you must determine whether you can live with the paychecks and stubs that this package is programmed to produce (which means designing and ordering new paychecks) or whether you must have the check printer reprogrammed (the vendor may do this for you —check the price and guarantee of any software changes done by the vendor). With your paychecks, the system should also produce a payroll report, showing all the income and deduction items to appear on each check, along with subtotals and a grand total.

The next most useful category of reports is for the government, of which there seems to be a surfeit. Among these are the W-2 forms, the quarterly 941-A report, and the unemployment tax report. A big plus for the right size company are equal employment opportunity reports for the government, drawn from the ethnic, sex, and position code fields.

Finally, the system should produce an employee report showing all the personal information and the MTD/QTD/YTD fields.

Process. The payroll files generally contain the most sensitive information on your system. Therefore you should carefully check out any

OPT	KEY	LINK	DESCRIPTION
			Federal tax tables
			State tax tables
			Local tax tables

Figure 47. Payroll tax tables.

security features built into the programs to prevent unauthorized access and alteration of the various fields. The best way to control access is by password, which any payroll system program would require before allowing entry to the files. On small, diskette-based systems, physical security of the diskettes is generally all that is required. For systems with hard disks, more elaborate precautions are needed.

As with the general ledger, end-of-period (month, quarter, and year) processing is a critical function. The appropriate fields are rolled into other fields and are zeroed. When evaluating a payroll package, run through the complete accounting cycle yourself to see how easy or difficult it is to make an error, and if you do, what facilities are available to correct your procedural errors. Generally, trying to reverse some action is as difficult with payroll as it is with the general ledger.

Inputs.   The employee master file can be created from an employment application. Timecards are the most widely used form of payroll input. A system that processes exceptions is highly desirable. Under this type of operation, salaried people and others whose paychecks remain the same from week to week are paid each time the payroll is run. The system should accept exceptions to any paycheck, such as additional commission income, garnishments, bonuses, sick, vacation, and holiday pay, etc. Eliminating the need to continually input the same information week after week for a given employee results in considerable savings in clerical time, as well as eliminating the most common source of error for payroll systems.

Payroll is inherently a batch processing type of system (as opposed to transaction-oriented or on-line). Therefore, the input programs should not only produce a complete audit trail of all input activity, but should also prompt the data entry clerk for batch totals to verify that the inputs have all been correct.

DATABASES AND DATABASE MANAGEMENT SYSTEMS (DBMS)

The development and implementation of the database concept has been one of the biggest changes to hit the field of data processing in the last 10 years. I do not know of any database management system currently available for small business systems, but I'm sure they're in the development stage and may even be available by the time this book is printed. Though up to now they have been associated mostly with large-scale systems and more recently with minicomputers, there is no inherent reason why the capabilities of micro-based systems cannot support a database. So what is a database, anyway?

This is a very difficult question to answer. If you are going to use a turnkey system, the organization of the data in your files should be transparent to you. That is, you should never have cause to know or care how the programs are stashing away and fetching back all your information. However, since I believe that there is a good chance that the next 10 years of software development will center around databases and that most of the data may eventually be converted to the database format, some introduction to them is necessary to complete your introduction to applications software.

If you look back at the file layouts for the order entry/invoicing system, you'll see several links to other files in each layout. These links don't actually exist in the files; they are logical links. When you read in one invoice record, your program must extract the bill-to-customer number, and, using this term as a key, get the customer information from another file. Figure 48 shows this traditional approach to information management. The items in the circles are abbreviations for different items of data -- L-NAME for last name, CUST-NUM for customer number, and so on.

In a database management system (shown schematically in Figure 49), the concept of individual files is replaced by a single giant file called a database, in which various data-items are grouped into data-sets. Whereas the files in the accounts receivable system may be of a different format than those of the payables system — requiring different programming techniques or conventions to access them — all the data-items and data-sets in a database share a common definition. They can easily be linked and relinked to form different views of the same information. Where the programs in your system may work well doing the things for which they were designed, the addition of any new information to the files will make it necessary to change all the programs that look at that file. This means that once you've designed the file layouts, that system is pretty much set in concrete.

For example, after you implement your inventory system, you'll be thrilled for about 2 weeks and then say, "I wish I could see a report that would show my usage of items by supplier. . . ." or something similar. Of course, you can have your report. All you have to do is hire a programmer to decipher the files and programming conventions in your canned software and write a new program linking two unrelated sets of data. "But," the programmer-for-hire will tell you, "you don't have the vendor number attached to the inventory item, so there's no way for me to know who sold you what. I could add vendor to your inventory file, but then you'd have to have all your inventory programs rewritten to reflect the existence of this new field." He or she then offers to do it for stock options and a company car.

Now, if you had implemented your systems on a database, the addition

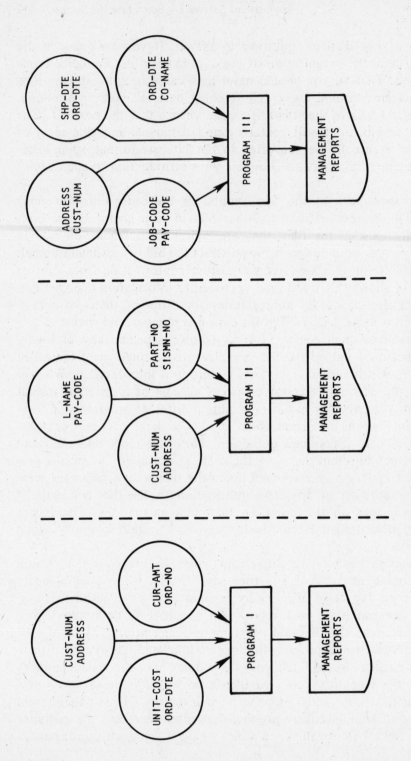

Figure 48. Traditional approach to information management.

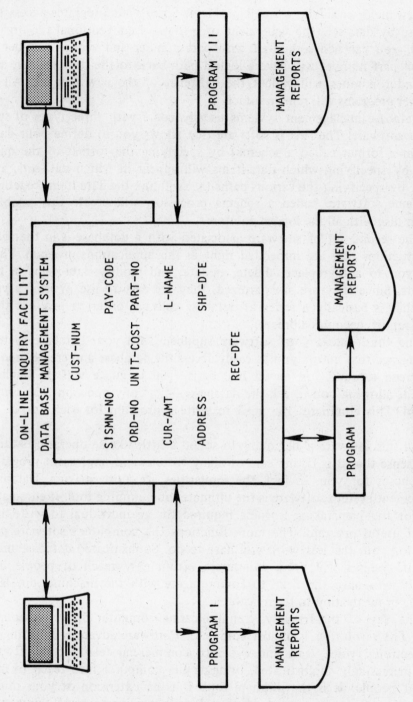

Figure 49. Database approach to information management.

DATA BASE MANAGEMENT SYSTEM

ON-LINE INQUIRY FACILITY

CUST-NUM   PAY-CODE

SISMN-NO   ORD-NO   UNIT-COST   PART-NO

CUR-AMT   L-NAME

ADDRESS   REC-DTE   SHP-DTE

PROGRAM III

MANAGEMENT REPORTS

PROGRAM II

MANAGEMENT REPORTS

PROGRAM I

MANAGEMENT REPORTS

of a new field would be a small problem. Since your programs access the database by data-set (the equivalent of a file in a conventional file organization), you can add a data-set with part number and vendor number in it. Each part number will have a logical path back to the item master, and the vendor number will reflect the existence of the new data-set. All of the other programs will remain intact.

Database management systems usually come with three types of supporting software. The first is software that allows you to define your database (in a format called a schema) by specifying the format of the data-items, by specifying which data-items will appear in which data-sets, and finally, by specifying the various paths that will link the data-items together. This same software, called a schema processor, will create the database on your disk with all the logical pointers.

The second set of software associated with a database is in the form of instructions that are imbedded right in the applications program. They allow you to add, replace, delete, update, and modify data-items in the data-sets. Since they are standardized, they are easy to use. Writing a program that is basically a series of database calls, in order to produce that special report, becomes a breeze.

The third category of software supplied with your database system is a language that allows you to easily access the database and create reports and screen retrievals on an ad hoc basis. The language will be English-oriented, allowing you to ask the database almost any question that comes to mind. This eliminates the need to write a program for each output required.

All this software is beginning to sound a little like an operating system in the sense that it is taking care of many tedious and unpleasant programming chores for you. In fact, the similarities are quite striking. Database management system software is the ultimate programming tool. It eliminates much of the painstaking learning required for an individual to write any kind of useful program. The more functions the computer's software performs for you, the less work you have to do. Sophisticated database management systems will bring computers within easy reach of people like yourself who have the need to communicate with the machine, but lack the time or motivation to learn how.

The day of the friendly, communicating computer draws closer and closer. The revolution is almost complete. Hardware advances are bringing the electronic voice, ear, and eye into commercial feasibility. Software grows increasingly sophisticated, bringing the computer into reach of millions of people. It is the ultimate tool. It is an extension of your mind; an unfailing electronic servant. More and more it relieves you of the mental tedium that eats up so much of your time, leaving you free to do those things which the computer could never do — create, grow, appreciate, and love.

6

WHAT TO DO
UNTIL THE
COMPUTER COMES

How many times have you heard this small business tale of woe? "We did have a computer in here for about a year. Spent close to $100 thousand on it, too, but we never did get the thing to work right. Finally, we had to get rid of it."

As Winston Churchill said, "Those who refuse to learn the lessons of history are doomed to repeat it." If, after having gone this far in the book, your enthusiasm for automating is matched only by your fear of the unknown, read this chapter ver-ry carefully. It is my contention that most failures in the attempt to automate come from the inability to foresee the problems to be overcome and the kind of effort and resources needed to overcome them.

Nothing is more disheartening than to have a computer sit around in a business for 3 or 4 months not operating or not giving any results. Even though there is much work to be done before the system is delivered, the first impulse of most first-time computer users is to get the machine first and then figure out what to do with it.

Many of the most serious problems you will encounter can be anticipated by following the installation planning guide that follows — a plan adapted from the excellent installation planning guide offered by ASK Computer Services of Los Altos, California, to their customers, prior to the delivery of their systems. The purpose of the guide is to eliminate the "seat-of-pants" approach taken of necessity by most new users of small business systems. They solve the problems one by one as they arise, never knowing how or if the solution to one problem is spawning many new ones in the unforeseeable future. As in all of your business endeavors, planning is the unquestionable key to your success.

1. *Define Your Requirements*
   a. *Examine current systems.* Before you call the first vendor, look at the first advertisement, or go to your first trade show, sit down with a blank pad of paper and write down all of the current manual systems you now employ — payables, receivables, inventory, customer mailing lists, shipping procedures, petty cash, everything you can think of. Now rate each of these systems in two ways: First, how is it working today? If it's not doing too well, make some brief notes on what you think the problems are — too much paperwork, inadequate training, clerical error, not enough feedback, inaccurate information, etc.

      Now, rerate each system assuming that the size of your business will double in 2 years. How well do they hold up? What's wrong with them under the increased business activity? Can these problems be solved by altering the manual system?

      Study this sheet carefully and ask yourself the $5 thousand–$100 thousand questions: Do I need a computer? Do I really need to automate? Can I solve these problems by upgrading my manual systems and also provide for growth to two or three times my present level? Knowing what you now know about small business systems, the good news and the bad news, I would say your chances of going any farther into the realm of data processing are exactly 50–50. If you decide at this point to defer or abandon the project, congratulations. You just saved yourself a boatload of money and headaches. Buy everyone a round of drinks and send them home for the day.

      If, on the other hand, you conclude that a small business system is the answer, also congratulations. You have quite probably found the one tool that will enable you to survive your current problems and all the new ones that accrue to a rapidly-growing business. (You see, I really am very procomputer. I'm just trying to be fair.) Read on.

   b. *Configure software needs.* Using the primal system again, start by making a list of the outputs you would like from a system. They will fall into broad categories covered by the popular business packages — payables, receivables, payroll, etc. In addition to this, you may have a specialized need, something particular to your business, which will have to be custom programmed.

   c. *Configure hardware needs.* Proceeding around the primal system diagram, try to estimate roughly the sizes of the files you will be storing — how many customers, vendors, outstanding invoices, payables, employees, sales orders, general ledger accounts, transactions per month of all types, etc. If you can't tell from this whether you will need mini-floppies, standard floppies, Winchesters, hard disks, or something else, at least you'll have answers to the questions the sales people will ask when trying to determine your storage requirements.

Inputs will be pretty much limited to terminals. The big question here is, will you need more than one? If so, the processor must be capable of handling multiple terminals — both the hardware and the operating system.

d. *Get a formal price quotation for hardware and software.* Getting this done includes the software evaluation procedure outlined earlier. This procedure will cut down on the number of quotations you will get because you'll be such a pain in the neck that many sales people won't want to bother with you. What you'll be left with are the good systems; the ones the sales people believe in.

e. *Present proposal to management.* If you're management, present the proposal to your partners or immediate subordinates. Invite participation in this decision. It's a complex and difficult decision. More opinions at this point can only help to uncover factors you might have overlooked. Remember, everyone will be affected by this computer. Having their cooperation and support will ensure a successful implementation.

2. *Schedule Your System Implementation*
    a. *Order hardware and software.*   There's no turning back now.
    b. *Establish delivery dates.* Try to understand your supplier. This industry is hit sporadically with shortages caused by bad forecasting, quality control problems, component shortages, etc. Plan on the possibility that the delivery schedule will be slipped.

    If you are having software written for you, try to protect yourself with a performance clause inserted into the contract. I've never seen a piece of customized software delivered on time and bug-free. Your outstanding invoice is the greatest lever you have to make the supplier perform to specifications. In order to avoid conflict over what was specified, the supplier should provide you with complete software specification documentation for you to buy off, before they write a single line of code for you.

3. *Prepare Your Staff for the New System*
    a. *Select an operator and a backup operator.* Matching the skills and capabilities of the person to the job to be performed is as important here as it is in any position. If you have gone through the software selection procedure, you have a pretty good idea of how simple or complicated the various procedures are in the

software you have chosen. Choose your staff accordingly. Backup in staff is as important as backup of data. Be sure there is more than one person who knows each part of the operation.

b. *Plan schedule for data-gathering.* Once the system arrives, the initial implementation steps will require the input of a great deal of data that need to go in just once — the item master, the name and address files, the current balances on the general ledger accounts, etc. Have the source of all of this data identified and prepare a step-by-step plan for inputting before delivery. Your software supplier should be glad to help you with this task.

c. *Enroll operational people in classes.* Some vendors offer formal training for their systems. Some will charge a day's on-site consulting fee to talk to your employees about the system and give demonstrations. Plan on this expense when budgeting for your system. It will be money well spent.

4. *Prepare Your Data and Forms*
   a. *Gather and edit initial data for master files.* This is an excellent opportunity to do some housecleaning of your files — weed out the old customers and suppliers, check addresses and telephone numbers, etc. After all, you don't want to load up a fresh, clean database with a bunch of dirty data, do you?

   b. *Have data prekeyed.* If possible, have your data entered on whatever media your system supports before it is delivered. This is another of those time–consuming tasks that tend to reveal procedural problems, missing data, input bottlenecks, etc. It gives your data entry and operating people a chance to get familiar with the machine and to make mistakes before they really count. If you are converting from another system or a service bureau, you may be able to take this opportunity to get a conversion program written to convert your files from the old system to the new one.

   c. *Order preprinted forms.* This is another real schedule slipper. From design to delivery, forms can sometimes take 8 to 10 weeks. Hopefully, the software people can supply you with samples of preprinted forms for your invoices, statements, check and stubs, shippers — whatever you are going to have the system print. Try to avoid having to modify the software to fit your forms. Be adaptable. Avoid unnecessary programmer's fees and maintenance problems.

   d. *Order backup media.* Order lots of it. It's very cheap compared to the total price of your system and even cheaper compared to

the cost of reentering lost data that weren't backed up for lack
of media. Penny-wise, pound-foolish.

e. *Order paper for line printer and hard copy terminals.* There's
usually no problem here. It's a stock item now in your neighbor-
hood computer supply store — unless there's a paper shortage
(remember the last one?).

f. *Begin using new forms where possible.* Roll them into a typewriter and type on them. Your people will become accustomed
to using them and reading them. Problems with the forms and
your manual support systems may come to the fore, and it will
ease the anxiety that always accompanies the transition to automated systems.

g. *Prepare test data.* When your computer first arrives, you will
want to check out the operation of the software and train the
people who will be using it. You will also have questions from
time to time about the effect of a certain operation or the way
a program updates a file. I have found that despite the trouble
that preparing test data can be, it pays off many times over for
months after your system is delivered. Either invent some data
or use some of your live data to build test data for every file you
will be using. This will provide a "no-penalty" place for you and
your people to make mistakes and try out new procedures.

5. *Prepare the Physical Site for Your Computer*
   a. *Set aside a place for the computer.* It should be in a low-noise,
   low-traffic area. If it is intended for use by several people for
   inquiries, make it accessible.

   b. *Prepare site.* Computers are often troubled by the close proximity
   of telephone switching systems and electrically "noisy" machinery
   and appliances. Devices that draw a lot of power upon start-up
   can cause voltage drops in the AC power line of your machine,
   causing it to fail. Problems of this type can be overcome by putting
   an inexpensive line filter between your computer and its AC source.
   If possible, plug your printer into a different outlet than the processor uses.

      Integrated systems generally require at most two outlets, one
   for the computer and one for the printer. If you are putting together your own components, you may need as many as 6 outlets.
   Plan for this by having an outlet strip and as many line filters
   as necessary on hand.

      Computer furniture is gaining popularity now. It's not cheap,
   but if you find it pleasing aesthetically, go for it. It would be

best, of course, to have somebody work at it for a couple of hours to see just how comfortable and functional it is. My personal preference is for long folding tables: They're cheap, sturdy, and have lots of room for spreading out printed output and source documents.

Operating a computer requires a high degree of neatness and precision. Make this easy by providing inexpensive accessories like diskette organizers and output binders.

6. *Hardware and Software Installation and Checkout*
   a. *Accept delivery of hardware.* Examine shipment. Use the same procedure as for delivery of any fixed sheet.

   b. *Install and test hardware.* Hopefully, the manufacturer will have provided you with some diagnostic programs to check out the processor, the memory, the printer, and to exercise the disks. Otherwise, the only thing you can do is:

   c. *Install and test the software.* Use your test data to create small test files — customers, invoices, inventory, whatever systems you are implementing. Run through the entire cycle, checking every program for accuracy and freedom from bugs. If you think it's necessary, type and copy off a bunch of bug reports like the one shown in Appendix E. Use it to report any bugs or problems to the manufacturer and file a copy for follow-up. You can also use it to document enhancements or changes you would like to see implemented.

7. *Train Staff in Using Software*
   a. *Set up user and management demonstration sessions.* Nothing is more upsetting to people than to have a computer move in to the company without being told about it. All the old myths about it taking away everyone's job, spying on people, and the like, are still alive and well. The object of this move is to demystify the computer.

   b. *Demonstrate software to all interested and affected personnel.* This is a tough job. Some people won't know what you're talking about. Some will be afraid. Some will be deliberately disruptive. At least one will spend all his or her time telling you why this system won't work. Try to outline to each function in the company exactly what the computer will do for them and how they can come to the computer for answers. Give them the feeling that they are in control, not being controlled.

   c. *Establish operating procedures.* The most important procedure is your backup cycle. Impress the operators with the critical nature of this operation. Threaten to hold their children hostage if it's not done right. Almost as important, of course, are the procedures for inputting data, running the reports, and updating the files. If you have the time and patience, have the procedures typed and placed in a binder by the computer with the manufacturer's operating manual for reference by the operators.

d. *Train operators*. This should be done on a one-to-one basis. Start with the test data. Check all their work very carefully the first few live sessions. If they are making a consistent mistake, it's probably due to something you forgot to tell them. The most important thing here is to establish a "no-penalty" atmosphere for your operators; one in which they will be encouraged to ask questions.

8. *Load Master Files with Data, If This Has Not Already Been Done Previous to Delivery*

Also, load file with the current data — quantities on hand, general ledger, account month-to-date, and year-to-date totals.

9. *Run Parallel With Old System*

This is extremely important, particularly if your auditors are fussy. More to the point, you'll want some confirmation that your system is operating correctly. If you can handle it, I recommend running 2 full months in parallel. This will mean some extra work for your people while they are supporting two systems, but if they have been properly prepped, they will understand the need for this. Don't assume that discrepancies between the old and new systems are due to the computer. Many a manual system has been known to be wrong.

10. *Complete Cutover to New System*

When you have run parallel long enough to satisfy yourself that you are not going to destroy your business, discontinue the old system. Then make plans to expand your business.

CONCLUSION

For almost every business person, automating a small business is a brand new experience. As such, it is obviously not possible to know in advance what procedure to follow, what steps to take and in what order, and what details are important and which ones are trivial. As I hope I have demonstrated in this chapter, and in this whole book for that matter, there are two things one can do to minimize the hazards and pitfalls of automating and maximize one's chances for success and reward — education and planning. By educating yourself, you gain the vocabulary you need to allow fruitful interactions with those in the industry who stand ready to help you. Planning ahead will allow an orderly transition from the manual mode to the more efficient, productive, and profitable automated business in your future.

GLOSSARY

ASCII — The American Standard Code for Information Interchange; the most popular convention for the representation of alphanumeric data on storage devices, such as disk and tape, in a computer's memory, and for transmission of data between computers or computers and peripheral devices. (See EBCDIC.)

Assembler — A program that translates an assembly language source program into machine language.

Assembly language — A programming language in which, generally, one line of source code is translated into one machine language instruction. Assembly languages are generally written for a specific machine, and the programs are therefore difficult to transfer between machines.

Audit trail — A record, either on printed output or stored on a magnetic medium, such as disk or tape, which details all of the activity that has taken place in an applications program. It can be used to recreate data that have been lost due to machine failure or to determine how certain data in the files were created.

Backup — The creation of copies of data files for the purpose of being able to recreate the data in the event of machine failure or human operating errors that destroy the original data.

BASIC — A popular programming language for small computers; it's simple to learn and use. Although the language is slightly different from one manufacturer to the next, the bulk of the rules of syntax are the same, making it easy to move BASIC language programs from one machine to another.

Batch processing — A method of processing data where transactions are accumulated manually over a period of time and are then all input into the computer at the same time. (See on-line processing.)

Bi-directional — Refers to printers that can print both from left to right and right to left.

Binary — The base two numbering system that represents all numbers as combinations of the two numbers zero and one. All computers use binary internally in the storage and representation of information, as well as instructions.

Bit — A contraction of binary digit, the fundamental unit of information in computer systems. It can have a value of zero or one. All other alphanumeric data is made of combinations of bits.

Byte — Eight bits, certain combinations of which are used by the computer to represent alphanumeric information of program instructions. (See ASCII.)

Cassette — A serial access storage device similar to audio cassettes and cassette records used for music recording and playback. They are used by small computer systems for the storage of data or programs.

Character printer — A printer that prints one character of information at a time. (See line printer.)

Chip — A slang term for integrated circuit.

Circuit card (or circuit board) — A plastic board with electronic components mounted on one side and the circuit printed in copper on the back. They plug into computers through connectors printed on the edge of the card and are easily removed and replaced, making computer maintenance faster and easier.

COBOL — The Common Business Oriented Language; a high level language generally transferrable from one machine to another. It is designed to read like English prose and is therefore very much self-documenting.

Command — See instruction.

Compiler — A manufacturer–supplied piece of software that is responsible for translating an applications program from the source language into machine language.

Concurrent execution — Use of the same computer resources (processor, programs, data) by more than one user at the same time.

CRT — Cathode Ray Tube; the "TV screen" portion of a terminal upon which data are displayed.

Database — A collection of data organized and stored by a DBMS to provide convenient access to the data.

DBMS — DataBase Management System; a collection of software that provides a user with the tools to store and retrieve data of various types in an easy and economical fashion.

Disk — A random access magnetic storage device in which data is recorded in circular tracks on the surface of the disk.

Diskette — See floppy disk.

Distributed Data Processing — Refers to a combination of hardware and software that allows independent processors with their own programs, terminals, printers, and storage devices to share the data of other processors or a centrally located data file.

Dot matrix — A method of forming characters of printed output from a matrix of dots, usually 5 × 7 or 7 × 9.

Drive — Common term for the mechanical device that reads and writes data on magnetic media — most commonly, tape drive and disk (or floppy disk) drive.

Dual density — A relatively new development in floppy disks that doubles the amount of data that can be stored on a diskette by doubling the number of tracks on the diskette.

EBCDIC — Extended Binary Coded Decimal Interchange Code; used by IBM and IBM-compatible hardware for the representation of data. (See ASCII.)

Field — One item of data within a record that has a specific meaning, such as the social-security-number field, the address field, or the quantity-on-hand field.

File — A collection of records.

Floppy disk — A magnetic data storage device made of a circular piece of plastic with a magnetic surface, either 5¼″ or 8″ in diameter, enclosed in a protective envelope, upon which data is stored in circular pattern or tracks; also the disk drive into which the floppy disk is inserted.

FORTRAN — FORmula TRANslator; a high level language originally designed for mathematical and scientific applications, now finding wider and wider use in small business systems.

Hard copy — Printed output.

Hard disk — Magnetic data storage device similar in principle to the floppy disk, except that the disk itself is rigid and not flexible, and the density of data, the capacity of the disk, the data transfer rate between disk and computer, and the price are all higher.

Instruction — One action taken by a computer, such as add two numbers, compare one number with another, or transfer control to a different part of a program.

Instruction set — All of the commands that a given computer can execute.

Integrated circuit — An electronic device in which the components have been miniaturized to the point where thousands of them fit on a chip of silicon only a quarter-inch square.

Interpreter — A program that can read a source language program, such as one written in BASIC, and cause the computer to execute instructions that carry out the commands in the source language program. Unlike a compiler, the interpreter does not translate the source program into machine language before executing it.

I/O — An abbreviation for Input/Output.

ISAM, KSAM — Indexed or Keyed Sequential Access Method; a way of storing and retrieving data based on the value of one of the fields of the record known as the "key" or "index" field.

Keyboard — The typewriter-like device, usually associated with a CRT, that allows entry of information into a computer.

Line printer — A printer that prints a whole line of information at one time. (See character printer.)

Machine language — The only language that a computer really understands; it is entirely numeric and is made up of the numeric codes that represent the sequence of instructions the computer executes.

Microprocessor — An integrated circuit that contains all of the functions (logic, arithmetic, and control) of a computer.

Object program — A program in machine language; generally the output of a compiler. Object code is a synonym.

Off-line — Not connected directly to the computer system.

On-line — Connected directly to the computer system and available for access by same.

On-line processing — Data processing method whereby data are processed at the same time as they are input. (See batch processing.)

Operating system — The traffic cop of the computer; an elaborate program that is responsible for starting and stopping programs and scheduling and allocating the computer's resources among competing users.

Peripherals — I/O devices attached to a processor; printers, disk drives, keyboards, and CRTs are all examples of peripheral devices.

Port — A place where a peripheral device may be plugged into a computer.

Program — A sequence of instructions that commands a computer to perform a step-by-step procedure.

RAM — Random Access Memory; term most often used to refer to the computer's memory. It can be both written into and read out of.

Random access — Data access method whereby any record in a file can be directly stored or retrieved based on a key or index value. (See sequential access, ISAM, and KSAM.)

Record — A collection of data items that are logically related. All the records of a given type are referred to as a file.

ROM — Read Only Memory; special kind of memory in a computer containing programs that cannot be changed by the user.

RS232 — A standard plug that allows terminals, printers, and other peripheral devices to be plugged into a computer, even though they may be from different manufacturers.

Sector — A section of a track on a disk.

Sequential or serial access — Data storage and retrieval method in which the data are read from the device in sequence (no jumping from one place in the file to another) or written to the device in such a manner that each record written is added only to the end of the file.

Software — General term that applies to all programming.

Source program — A computer program in the language that the programmer originally wrote it. It must be translated into an object program (machine language) before the computer can execute it.

Terminal — A device usually consisting of a CRT and a keyboard, connected or on-line to a computer system, used for entering data, programs, or commands into the computer and retrieving and displaying data or programs from the computer.

Thrashing — A term that refers to an excessive amount of time being spent by an operating system doing its job or managing the computer's resources. All the time the operating system is doing its job, no applications programs are executing.

Track — A circular data storage area on a disk.

Utility program — Program that performs data transfer from one device or medium to another, sorting, or other tasks common to all data processing systems.

Winchester — A term referring to a type of hard disk drive in which the disk itself is not removable but is sealed into the drive itself.

APPENDICES

SYSTEM PRICING WORKSHEET: HARDWARE

A. Computer System

    Processor and terminal $ _____

    Extra terminals   ____ @$ ____   _____

    Additional memory   ____ k   _____

    Disk and tape drives:

        Floppies   ____ @$ ____ /drive   _____

        Winchesters   ____ @$ ____ /drive   _____

        Hard disks   ____ @$ ____ /drive   _____

        Cartridge   ____ @$ ____ /drive   _____

        Cassette drive   ____ @$ ____ /drive   _____

    Printers:

        Matrix   _____

        Impact   _____

        Line   _____

        Paper catcher/stand   _____

    Cables and connectors   _____

    Interface boards   _____

    Total hardware $ _____

B. Supplies

    Recording media (disks, tapes, etc.)   _____

Stock paper $ _____

Forms (invoices, paychecks, etc.)   _____

Total supplies $ _____

C. Furniture

Desk(s), stand, or work station
   for computer and/or terminal(s)   _____

Chair(s)   _____

Anti-static floor pad(s)   _____

Tape/disk storage   _____

Total furniture $ _____

B

SYSTEM PRICING WORKSHEET: SOFTWARE

Systems:

    Operating system $ _____

    Utilities   _____

Applications:

    General ledger   _____

    Accounts receivable   _____

    Accounts payable   _____

    Inventory control   _____

    Payroll   _____

    Order entry   _____

    Purchasing   _____

    Database management system   _____

    Custom software   _____

    Software modifications   _____

Total software $ _____

C

SYSTEM PRICING WORKSHEET: IMPLEMENTATION

Shipping $ _____

Data conversion   _____

Training courses   _____

In-house training   _____

Forms design   _____

Insurance   _____

Consultants   _____

Overhead (utilities, floor space)   _____

Total implementation $ _____

D

SYSTEM EVALUATION, PURCHASE, AND IMPLEMENTATION CHECKLIST

- Define your requirements
    - Examine current systems
    - Configure software needs
    - Configure hardware needs
    - Get formal price quotation for hardware and software
    - Present proposal to management
- Schedule your system implementation
    - Order hardware and software
    - Establish delivery dates
- Prepare staff for the new system
    - Select operators and backup operators
    - Plan schedule for data gathering
    - Enroll operational people in classes
- Prepare data and forms
    - Gather and edit initial data for master files
    - Have data prekeyed
    - Order preprinted forms
    - Order backup media
    - Order paper for printer and hard copy terminals
    - Begin using new forms where possible
    - Prepare test data
- Prepare physical site for your computer
    - Set aside a place for the computer
    - Prepare site
- Hardware and software installation and checkout
    - Accept delivery of hardware

- Install and test hardware
- Install and test software
- Train staff using software
  - Set up user and management demonstration sessions
  - Demonstrate software to all interested and affected personnel
  - Establish operating procedures
  - Train operators
- Load master files with data
- Run parallel with old system
- Complete cutover to new system

E

THE BUG REPORT

No software is totally free of bugs. Some are hard bugs that will cause the program to abort. Some are soft bugs — they won't cause the system to fail but they will produce erroneous results. Finally, there are operational bugs — things go wrong because of errors in operating procedures. This may be the fault of unclear documentation by the software vendor or it may be your error.

In any case, it is essential that these problems be reported to the vendor in an organized fashion, providing as much information as possible, and that follow-up be done to ensure that the vendor responds satisfactorily to your problem. Use either the bug report presented here or design your own, but make sure everyone knows where it is and how to use it so that the form will be filled out at the time the problem occurs.

A sequence number, date, and a space for the vendor to write in a resolution to your problem will help ensure a timely and effective resolution to your problem.

SOFTWARE BUG REPORT   SEQ. #: _____

Your name: Company name:

Address: City, State, Zip:

Phone number: Date:

What program were you trying to run?

What went wrong?

What was the last prompt you responded to?

Were you able to duplicate the problem?

Any other information?

Supporting materials attached: ____ Program output

                                                ____ Printouts

                                                ____ Disk or tape

                                                ____ Other

For Vendor's Reply

Resolution:

F

SOFTWARE MODIFICATION FORM

In the very likely event that you will someday try to modify your own software, it is imperative that an accurate and meticulous record of every change to every line of code be documented. Many vendors will simply refuse to look at their programs once they have been modified. However, many will tolerate and even support your changes if they are well documented. Nothing irritates a software vendor more than having to spend a lot of time and money tracking down a software problem only to find that it was due to a modification that the user made.

Before modifying any of your own software, make a copy of the original program. If you run into difficulties making your modification, or subtle errors start creeping into your processing after you have implemented a change, you can always copy back the original program, thus eliminating one possible source of the errors.

SOFTWARE MODIFICATIONS FORM

Program name:

Description:

Programmer:

Date of change:

Purpose of change:

Description of changes by line number:
(Show both old line and new line)

The old program was saved under the name:

G

FLOWCHARTING
SYMBOLS

1. Process

   Written inside this symbol will be a step in a program ("add quantity received to quantity on hand"), a direction to a user ("make backup copy"), or perhaps the name of a program (in the case of a system flowchart).

2. Disk file

   This symbol represents any kind of a file on a rotating, random access device: floppy disk, hard disk, or Winchester type drive.

3. Decision

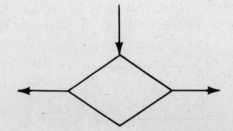

Written inside this symbol will be a condition to be evaluated by either a program or a user ("A=B?," "quantity on hand 10?"). The result of this evaluation will determine which of the two paths to follow out of this symbol. Most often the condition is couched in terms that yield a yes/no answer.

4. Display

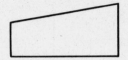

This symbol indicates that the data or item(s) written inside the symbol are to be displayed on a CRT.

5. Keyboard input

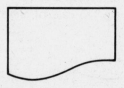

This symbol indicates the entry of data through the keyboard.

6. Document

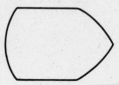

This symbol indicates either a source document that contains data to be input into a system or a printed report — the output of a program.

7. Tape

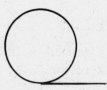

This symbol indicates that tape is to be used as an input or output medium. The name(s) of the file(s) will appear inside the symbol.

8. Punched card

This symbol is seldom used, as punched cards are not a popular input medium for small systems.

9. Start/stop marker

This symbol indicates the beginning or end of a program or process — the words START or STOP will appear inside this symbol.

INDEX

NOTES

NOTES

NOTES

NOTES

NOTES

NOTES

NOTES

NOTES